P9-DCN-299

THROUGH MANY WINDOWS

ARTHUR GORDON

THROUGH MANY WINDOWS

Guideposts

CARMEL • NEW YORK 10512

"The Bargain," originally titled "Dialogue in the Dark," and "A Reason for Living," originally "Dead Duck," were first published respectively in the September, 1942, and the March, 1952, issues of *Esquire* magazine.

"The Signal" is reprinted by permission of *Guideposts* magazine, which first published it under the title of "The Secret Signal." Copyright © 1952, renewed 1980, by Guideposts Associates, Inc., Carmel, NY 10512.

Grateful appreciation is expressed to the above publications and to the following magazines for permission to reprint in this volume the stories that originally appeared in these publications: *Better Homes & Gardens, Collier's Magazine, McCall's Magazine, Redbook Magazine, The Saturday Evening Post, This Week* magazine and *Woman's Home Companion*.

Library of Congress Cataloging in Publication Data

Gordon, Arthur.
  Through many windows.

  I. Title.
PS3557.0653T5 1983   813'.54   82-12308
ISBN 0-8007-1319-2

This Guideposts edition is published by
special arrangement with Fleming H. Revell Company.

FOR
the lioness
and all the cubs

Contents

If I take the wings of the morning,
and dwell in the uttermost parts of the sea;
Even there shall thy hand lead me,
and thy right hand shall hold me.

Psalms 139:9, 10

Preface

Many years ago a small boy found himself kept in bed for long periods of time by a series of ear infections. No antibiotics came to the rescue in those days. So there he sat, with tufts of cotton poking disconsolately out of his ears, but not too unhappy because he had an unlimited supply of books. No radio, no television. Just books. All sorts of books. Every kind of books.

He also had a remarkable aunt. She was a compact, gray-haired little woman with warm brown eyes and an irresistible laugh. She was a national celebrity, actually: founder of the Girl Scouts of America. But the boy knew little of this. All he knew was that there was something special about her. For one thing, she was quite deaf, and this made her sympathize with the boy's ear troubles. More than that, she had the gift of passing effortlessly through the barriers that separate grown-ups from children, perhaps because in some ways she had never ceased being a child herself.

Her visits were a joy because she was an incurable romantic. While the boy listened with closed eyes, she sang old ballads with creaky tunes and told him blood-chilling ghost stories. She could read palms and interpret dreams. Sometimes, if boredom threatened, she would go over to a corner and stand on her head. Folklore remedies fascinated her; once she brought a pipe to the boy's bedside and smoked it furiously into his aching ears. It did no good, but it did no harm either and certainly was preferable to the dreaded doctors with their relentless probes and baleful reflectors on their heads.

This magical aunt and the boy had a game they had invented, a kind of enchanted daydream. In the dream they were the sole occupants of a great stone tower, foursquare, surrounded by a moat. No one could get in, because the drawbridge was always raised. No one could get out, either, but this didn't trouble the two occupants because the tower had four tall windows facing the outer world. Each looked out on a different landscape, and through them it was possible to see stories happening. Any story you wanted. Any story at all.

If you looked to the north, for example, the countryside was a cold, pale blue. You could count on finding witches and wizards, dragons and demons, vampires and banshees. All the trolls and giants of fairy tales were in the north country. Princesses too.

To the east were the adventurers: highwaymen and outlaws, men against the sea. Warriors clashed endlessly: crusaders and Saracens, longbowmen and crossbowmen, pirates and corsairs, knights in armor with the sun glinting on visors and lance tips. Somebody was always fighting somebody in the view from the east window.

To the south the terrain was gentle and so were the stories: faithful dogs, noble horses, people who solved all problems and dreamed happy dreams. The boy's aunt said that in the south country the lanes were full of honeysuckle and that you could smell it if you tried hard enough. The boy tried very hard and found that it was so.

Through the west window one could see any story happening so long as it happened in verse. So that was where you looked if you wanted to ride with Paul Revere, or shiver at "The Skeleton in Armor," or feel the icy breakers lash the dismasted hulk of the *Hesperus*, or fall heroically dead like Napoleon's brave young soldier at Ratisbon.

In a way, the west window was the one the boy liked best, because in stories viewed from there the words had rhythms that burned themselves into his memory and made him see everything that happened with marvelous clarity. Among the jumbled books of verse was an old red copy (the red came off on your hands) of Macaulay's *Lays of Ancient Rome*, and when his aunt read from it, the boy felt as if the familiar bedroom dissolved and left him standing stern-faced with Horatius at the bridge over the Tiber, watching the rolling dust cloud that marked the approach of the Tuscan army:

> And nearer still and nearer,
> Now through the gloom appears,
> Far to left and far to right
> In broken gleams of dark blue light,
> The long array of helmets bright,
> The long array of spears.

Broken gleams of dark blue light. . . . Watching from his magic window, the boy felt his scalp tingle with the music and the mystery of words.

Later on, long after his aunt had departed on her final adventure, the boy understood the analogy of the tower, just as she had known he would. "Well, of course," he could almost hear her saying, "each of us looks out on life through windows of our own choosing, and each of us must try to interpret the scenes and images that come into view."

So the memory of the great stone tower never quite left the boy, and as he grew older he began to try to be a teller of tales himself, sometimes just for fun, sometimes because looking through the windows of imagination seemed to make reality more vivid and more comprehensible.

In the pages that follow, you'll find a handful of those tales, and a few backstage comments about them. Please don't look for neat categories or crisp organization. What you'll discover is more like a patchwork quilt. Some of the patches are more skillfully cut and sewn than others. But in all of them, I think, the little boy with the cotton in his ears is still there, peering out the tall windows, still looking for broken gleams of light.

A wise man once said that the best writing is full of lies that tell the truth.

The boy in the tower wouldn't quarrel with that.

ARTHUR GORDON

I

Life is a fascinating, challenging, complex business—everyone knows that. Everyone also knows that it's full of snarls, tangles, loose ends, puzzlements, and things that don't make sense. That's why most of us can't help wishing, now and then, that a magician would come along, wave his magic wand, and straighten things out a bit.

The storyteller's magic wand is a fragile little two-word question: *what if?* What if all these confusing things had happened differently? What if this apparently senseless sequence of events really made sense? What if this dilemma were solved in this surprising way?

What the storyteller is doing, of course, is looking through the windows of his imagination, trying to see things more clearly, hoping to help and enlighten and entertain others at the same time.

And sometimes, if the panes in the windows are clear enough, he does.

This *what if* approach can be applied to almost anything.

Once I knew a woman who was a truly fine sculptress. She never told me how she came to be a sculptress, and I never asked her. But one afternoon in her studio, wondering how so much beauty and power came out of such a fragile source, I caught a flash of color as sunlight struck a small object on her desk. And I asked myself, "What if that had something to do with it? Why else would she keep a thing like that?"

This is the way stories—even very short stories—are born.

Wings of the Morning

Years later, when her fame was secure, people would say to her sometimes, "What got you started, Troy? How did it all begin?"

She always smiled and shook her head, as if she didn't know. But sometimes her glance would stray to the fragment of greenish glass that she kept on her desk. She never told any of her admirers about that morning long ago. But she might have told them this. . . .

For one brief, soul-shattering moment, she thought he was dead. She stood there, appalled, hugging the loaf of bread her mother had sent her for. Beyond the curving dunes the sea lay placid and immense. Breakfast was waiting, the whole universe was in order, everything was as it should be except . . .

Except that here, on the little path that was her own private shortcut between home and the village, here were those unexpected feet, attached to a pair of legs that vanished into crumpled brown trousers, the trousers themselves disappearing under a flattened tent of dew-sodden newspaper that concealed—what?

She stood there, staring, remembering fragments of dinner table conversation that had passed between her mother and her Aunt Martha, dark mutterings about the riffraff seen along the beach nowadays, the rise of unemployment, of vandalism, of crime.

Secure in her ten-year-old world, Troy had paid little heed to this. But now, not a hundred yards from the house itself, here were these feet. Even as she looked, one of them twitched. Before she could move, an arm appeared—an arm in a tweed sleeve with frayed cuff. It pushed back the newspapers. Its owner sat up. Young? Old? Troy was too startled to care. The man looked startled, too. "Good morning," he said.

Troy took two steps backward. The voice was gentle; the words held no menace. But the sand-powdered hair, the dark shadow of beard—these were not reassuring.

"Go ahead," he said approvingly. "Run. I won't chase you. When I run, it's always away from something, these days." He turned his head stiffly. "That's your house over there, I suppose. And they sent you to the store for bread, right? Tell me—do people really still make toast for breakfast?"

Troy stood motionless, poised between flight and fascination. A creature who slept under damp newspapers, who ran away from things, who doubted the existence of toast for breakfast—such a phenomenon might be undesirable. It might even be dangerous. But it was not to be met with every day. Troy's heart thudded wildly, but she stood her ground.

The man untied one of his dismal shoes and emptied out a stream of sand. "I'm obliged to you," he said politely, "for waking me. Of course, at this hour I'm not quite myself. But I often wonder which self I really am—a jobless newspaper man, a frustrated poet, a fugitive from reality, or a victim of circumstance. I suppose *you* think I'm just a beachcomber. Well, maybe you're right."

Troy shook her head slowly, feeling a pang of guilt lance through her. If she did not return soon, her mother and her Aunt Martha would be worried; they would start looking for her. And if they found her here, like this . . .

He smiled at her, suddenly looking much younger. "I do know one thing. Whenever I go to bed without my supper, I'm apt to wake up a little light-headed. And when I'm light-headed, I talk too much. *You* don't say much do you? That's very wise. People who talk a lot seldom do anything. Take me, for example—no, better not take me. I wouldn't advise it. Let's talk about you. You're going to be *something.* I'm sure; otherwise you wouldn't be standing there—you'd be running. But you *don't* run, you see—and that's the difference between us."

Still she stared at him, puzzled, confused, but aware of a great sympathy, a great kindness, a warmth and understanding that she had never found at home—not since her father died.

"Come on," he said coaxingly, "tell me. What are you going to be? Actress, artist, musician, writer—or don't you know? How wonderful not to know, to have it all there ahead of you, fresh and shining, the whole untarnished future. But listen . . ."

He leaned forward, the lines deepening in his face. "I'll tell you a secret—one I learned too late. It all depends on beauty—how you see it, where you find it. People will tell you that—oh, that diamonds are beautiful and rare. And so they are. But here—," he scooped up a handful of sand—, "right here are a *million* diamonds, if you look close enough. Or this." He tossed her a fragment of glass, its edges worn smooth by sea and sand. "Worthless, they'll say. But hold it up to the light! It's green as emerald, mysterious as jade, smooth as jasper!"

A shadow moved between them; overhead drifted a questing gull. Bright-eyed it hovered, riding the silver stream of the wind. "There," he said, pointing, *"that's* what I mean. It's a matter of perception, don't you see? Of intensity of perception. You have to keep looking beyond the obvious. Not just a sea gull flying. Look for the pinions of hope, child! Look for the wings of the morning!"

The bird soared away. Troy said, in a small, frightened voice, "They're coming."

It was true; they had seen her. Down the veranda steps, skirts flying, came Aunt Martha. At her heels, still in pink dressing gown, was Troy's mother. Behind them both, ominous as Judgment Day, came Eliza from the kitchen with a cleaver in her hand.

Troy's companion hastily fitted on his shoe. "I'm sorry," he said, "but I warned you—I always run away." He ducked sideways through the golden sea wheat. Troy stood still and watched him go.

She did not move until Aunt Martha's hand was hard on her arm and Aunt Martha's voice was in her ears, metallic and shrill: "That horrible, horrible man . . . Telephone the police . . . What did he say to you—what did he try to *do?*"

"Nothing," Troy said. "Nothing."

But that was a lie, and she knew it was a lie, and in her tight-clenched fist was proof of it—the broken bit of sea-scoured glass that was green as emerald, mysterious as jade, smooth as jasper.

II

All my life I've been drawn to the sea. If there's any truth in the old saying that the Lord doesn't subtract from a man's life span the days spent fishing, I'll probably live as long as Methuselah. But salt-water fishing is a lot more than just pursuing fish: It's a reach for something else. In *Moby Dick*, Melville writes of "this sea, whose gently awful stirrings seem to speak of some hidden soul beneath." There *is* such a soul; I have felt it often. It can be as gentle and friendly and soothing as a lullaby. It can also be menacing and hostile and cruel.

The *what if* in this story must have hovered around the edge of my mind for a long time, and it's a simple one: What if, instead of man catching fish, fish catches man?

The details, you'll find, are authentic enough. In the past half century or so I must have thrown a cast net twenty thousand times. But authenticity isn't what this story is all about. What it's about is the deep, abiding respect—a respect close to fear—that all who truly know the sea have for it and for the creatures that dwell in it.

Oh, yes. You may love the sea with all your heart, and I do. But there are times when it will kill you if it can.

The Sea Devil

The man came out of the house and stood quite still, listening. Behind him, the lights glowed in the cheerful room, the books were neat and orderly in their cases, the radio talked importantly to itself. In front of him, the bay stretched dark and silent, one of the countless lagoons that border the coast where Florida thrusts its great green thumb deep into the tropics.

It was late in September. The night was breathless; summer's dead hand still lay heavy on the land. The man moved forward six paces and stood on the seawall. He dropped his cigarette and noted where the tiny spark hissed and went out. The tide was beginning to ebb.

Somewhere out in the blackness a mullet jumped and fell back with a sullen splash. Heavy with roe, they were jumping less often, now. They would not take a hook, but a practiced eyes could see the swirls they made in 'he glassy water. In the dark of the moon, a skilled man with a cast net might take half a dozen in an hour's work. And a big mullet makes a meal for a family.

The man turned abruptly and went into the garage, where his cast net hung. He was in his late twenties, wide shouldered and strong. He did not have to fish for a living, or even for food. He was a man who worked with his head, not with his hands. But he liked to go casting alone at night.

He liked the loneliness and the labor of it. He liked the clean taste of salt when he gripped the edge of the net with his teeth as a cast netter must. He liked the arching flight of sixteen pounds of lead and linen against the starlight, and the weltering crash of the net into the unsuspecting water. He liked the harsh tug of the retrieving rope around his wrist, and the way the net came alive when the cast was true, and the thud of captured fish on the floorboards of the skiff.

He liked all that because he found in it a reality that seemed to be missing from his twentieth-century job and from his daily life. He liked being the hunter, skilled and solitary and elemental. There was no conscious cruelty in the way he felt. It was the way things had been in the beginning.

The man lifted the net down carefully and lowered it into a bucket. He put a paddle beside the bucket. Then he went into the house. When he came out, he was wearing swimming trunks and a pair of old tennis shoes. Nothing else.

The skiff, flat-bottomed, was moored off the seawall. He would not go far, he told himself. Just to the tumbledown dock half a mile away. Mullet had a way of feeding around old pilings after dark. If he moved quietly, he might pick up two or three in one cast close to the dock. And maybe a couple of others on the way down or back.

He shoved off and stood motionless for a moment, letting his eyes grow accustomed to the dark. Somewhere out in the channel a porpoise blew with a sound like steam escaping. The man smiled a little; porpoises were his friends. Once, fishing in the Gulf, he had seen the charter-boat captain reach overside and gaff a baby porpoise through the sinewy part of the tail. He had hoisted it aboard, had dropped it into the bait well, where it thrashed around, puzzled and unhappy. And the mother had swum alongside the boat and under the boat and around the boat, nudging the stout planking with her back, slapping it with her tail, until the man felt sorry for her and made the captain let the baby porpoise go.

He took the net from the bucket, slipped the noose in the retrieving rope over his wrist, pulled the slipknot tight. It was an old net, but still serviceable; he had rewoven the rents made by underwater snags. He coiled the thirty-foot rope carefully, making sure there were no kinks. A tangled rope, he knew, would spoil any cast.

The basic design of the net had not changed in three thousand years. It was a mesh circle with a diameter of fourteen feet. It measured close to fifteen yards around the circumference and could, if thrown perfectly, blanket a hundred and fifty square feet of sea water. In the center of this radial trap was a small iron collar where the retrieving rope met the twenty-three separate drawstrings leading to the outer rim of the net. Along this rim, spaced an inch and a half apart, were the heavy lead sinkers.

The man raised the iron collar until it was a foot above his head. The net hung soft and pliant and deadly. He shook it gently, making sure that the drawstrings were not tangled, that the sinkers were hanging true. Then he eased it down and picked up the paddle.

The night was black as a witch's cat; the stars looked fuzzy and dim. Down to the southward, the lights of a causeway made a yellow necklace across the sky. To the man's left were the tangled roots of a mangrove swamp; to his right, the open waters of the bay. Most of it was fairly shallow, but there were channels eight feet deep. The man could not see the old dock, but he knew where it was. He pulled the paddle quietly through the water, and the phosphorescence glowed and died.

For five minutes he paddled. Then, twenty feet ahead of the skiff, a mullet jumped. A big fish, close to three pounds. For a moment it hung in the still air, gleaming dully. Then it vanished. But the ripples marked the spot, and where there was one there were often others.

The man stood up quickly. He picked up the coiled rope, and with the same hand grasped the net at a point four feet below the iron collar. He raised the skirt to his mouth, gripped it strongly with his teeth. He slid his free hand as far as it would go down the circumference of the net so that he had three points of contact with the mass of cordage and metal. He made sure his feet were planted solidly. Then he waited, feeling the tension that is older than the human race, the fierce exhilaration of the hunter at the moment of ambush, the atavistic desire to capture and kill and ultimately consume.

A mullet swirled, ahead and to the left. The man swung the heavy net back, twisting his body and bending his knees so as to get more upward thrust. He shot it forward, letting go simultaneously with rope hand and with teeth, holding a fraction of a second longer with the other hand so as to give the net the necesary spin, impart the centrifugal force that would make it flare into a circle. The skiff ducked sideways, but he kept his balance. The net fell with a splash.

The man waited for five seconds. Then he began to retrieve it, pulling in a series of sharp jerks so that the drawstrings would gather the net inward, like a giant fist closing on this segment of the teeming sea. He felt the net quiver, and knew it was not empty. He swung it, dripping over the gunwale, saw the broad silver side of the mullet quivering, saw too the gleam of a smaller fish. He looked closely to make sure no stingray was hidden in the mesh, then raised the iron collar and shook the net out. The mullet fell with a thud and flapped wildly. The other victim was an angel fish, beautifully marked, but too small to keep. The man picked it up gently and dropped it overboard. He coiled the rope, took up the paddle. He would cast no more until he came to the dock.

The skiff moved on. At last, ten feet apart, a pair of stakes rose up gauntly out of the night. Barnacle encrusted, they once had marked the approach from the main channel. The man guided the skiff between them, then put the paddle down softly. He stood up, reached for the net, tightened the noose around his wrist. From here he could drift down upon the dock. He could see it now, a ruined skeleton in the starshine. Beyond it a mullet jumped and fell back with a flat, liquid sound. The man raised the edge of the net, put it between his teeth. He would not cast at a single swirl, he decided; he would wait until he saw two or three close together. The skiff was barely moving. He felt his muscles tense themselves, awaiting the signal from the brain.

Behind him in the channel he heard the porpoise blow again, nearer now. He frowned in the darkness. If the porpoise chose to fish in this area, the mullet would scatter and vanish. There was no time to lose.

A school of sardines surfaced suddenly, skittering along like drops of mercury. Something, perhaps the shadow of the skiff, had frightened them. The old dock loomed very close. A mullet broke water just too far away; then another, nearer.

The man marked the spreading ripples and decided to wait no longer.

He swung back the net, heavier now that it was wet. He had to turn his head, but out of the corner of his eye he saw two swirls in the black water just off the starboard bow. They were about eight feet apart, and they had the sluggish oily look that marks the presence of something big just below the surface. His conscious mind had no time to function, but instinct told him that the net was wide enough to cover both swirls if he could alter the direction of his cast. He could not halt the swing, but he shifted his feet slightly and made the cast off-balance. He saw the net shoot forward, flare into an oval, and drop just where he wanted it.

Then the sea exploded in his face. In a frenzy of spray, a great horned thing shot like a huge bat out of the water. The man saw the mesh of his net against the mottled blackness of its body and he knew, in the split second in which thought was still possible, that those twin swirls had been made not by two mullet, but by the wing tips of the giant ray of the Gulf Coast, *Manta birostris*, also known as clam cracker, devil ray, sea devil.

The man gave a hoarse cry. He tried to claw the slipknot off his wrist, but there was no time. The quarter-inch line snapped taut. He shot over the side of the skiff as if he had roped a runaway locomotive. He hit the water head first and seemed to bounce once. He plowed a blinding furrow for perhaps ten yards. Then the line went slack as the sea devil jumped again. It was not a full-grown manta of the deep Gulf, but it was close to nine feet from tip to tip and it weighed over a thousand pounds. Up into the air it went, pearl-colored underbelly gleaming as it twisted in a frantic effort to dislodge the clinging thing that had fallen upon it. Up into the starlight, a monstrous survival from the dawn of time.

The water was less than four feet deep. Sobbing and choking, the man struggled for a foothold on the slimy bottom. Sucking in great gulps of air, he fought to free himself from the rope. But the slipknot was jammed deep into his wrist; he might as well have tried to loosen a circle of steel.

The ray came down with a thunderous splash and drove

forward again. The flexible net followed every movement, impeding it hardly at all. The man weighed a hundred and seventy-five pounds, and he was braced for the shock, and he had the desperate strength that comes from looking into the blank eyes of death. It was useless. His arm straightened out with a jerk that seemed to dislocate his shoulder; his feet shot out from under him; his head went under again. Now at last he knew how the fish must feel when the line tightens and drags him toward the alien element that is his doom. Now he knew.

Desperately he dug the fingers of his free hand into the ooze, felt them dredge a futile channel through broken shells and the ribbonlike sea grasses. He tried to raise his head, but could not get it clear. Torrents of spray choked him as the ray plunged toward deep water.

His eyes were of no use to him in the foam-streaked blackness. He closed them tight, and at once an insane sequence of pictures flashed through his mind. He saw his wife sitting in their living room, reading, waiting calmly for his return. He saw the mullet he had just caught, gasping its life away on the floorboards of the skiff. He saw the cigarette he had flung from the seawall touch the water and expire with a tiny hiss. He saw all these things and many others simultaneously in his mind as his body fought silently and tenaciously for its existence. His hand touched something hard and closed on it in a death grip, but it was only the sharp-edged helmet of a horseshoe crab, and after an instant he let it go.

He had been under water perhaps fifteen seconds now, and something in his brain told him quite calmly that he could last another forty or fifty and then the red flashes behind his eyes would merge into darkness, and the water would pour into his lungs in one sharp painful shock, and he would be finished.

This thought spurred him to a desperate effort. He reached up and caught his pinioned wrist with his free hand. He doubled up his knees to create more drag. He thrashed his body madly, like a fighting fish, from side to side. This did not disturb the ray, but now one of the great wings tore through the mesh, and the net slipped lower over the fins projecting like horns from below the nightmare head, and the sea devil jumped again.

And once more the man was able to get his feet on the bottom and his head above water, and he saw ahead of him the pair of ancient stakes that marked the approach to the channel. He knew that if he was dragged much beyond those stakes he would be in eight feet of water, and the ray would go down to hug the bottom as rays always do, and then no power on earth could save him. So in the moment of respite that was granted him, he flung himself toward them.

For a moment he thought his captor yielded a bit. Then the ray moved off again, but more slowly now, and for a few yards the man was able to keep his feet on the bottom. Twice he hurled himself back against the rope with all his strength, hoping that something would break. But nothing broke. The mesh of the net was ripped and torn, but the draw lines were strong, and the stout perimeter cord threaded through the sinkers was even stronger.

The man could feel nothing now in his trapped hand, it was numb; but the ray could feel the powerful lunges of the unknown thing that was trying to restrain it. It drove its great wings against the unyielding water and forged ahead, dragging the man and pushing a sullen wave in front of it.

The man had swung as far as he could toward the stakes. He plunged toward one and missed it by inches. His feet slipped and he went down on his knees. Then the ray swerved sharply and the second stake came right at him. He reached out with his free hand and caught it.

He caught it just above the surface, six or eight inches below high-water mark. He felt the razor-sharp barnacles bite into his hand, collapse under the pressure, drive their tiny slime-covered shell splinters deep into his flesh. He felt the pain, and he welcomed it, and he made his fingers into an iron claw that would hold until the tendons were severed or the skin was shredded from the bone. The ray felt the pressure increase with a jerk that stopped it dead in the water. For a moment all was still as the tremendous forces came into equilibrium.

Then the net slipped again, and the perimeter cord came down over the sea devil's eyes, blinding it momentarily. The great ray settled to the bottom and braced its wings against the mud and hurled itself forward and upward.

The stake was only a four-by-four of creosoted pine, and it was old. Ten thousand tides had swirled around it. Worms had bored; parasites had clung. Under the crust of barnacles it still had some heart left, but not enough. The man's grip was five feet above the floor of the bay; the leverage was too great. The stake snapped off at its base.

The ray lunged upward, dragging the man and the useless timber. The man had his lungs full of air, but when the stake snapped he thought of expelling the air and inhaling the water so as to have it finished quickly. He thought of this, but he did not do it. And then, just at the channel's edge, the ray met the porpoise coming in.

The porpoise had fed well this night and was in no hurry, but it was a methodical creature and it intended to make a sweep around the old dock before the tide dropped too low. It had no quarrel with any ray, but it feared no fish in the sea, and when the great black shadow came rushing blindly and unavoidably, it rolled fast and struck once with its massive horizontal tail.

The blow descended on the ray's flat body with a sound like a pistol shot. It would have broken a buffalo's back, and even the sea devil was half-stunned. It veered wildly and turned back toward shallow water. It passed within ten feet of the man, face down in the water. It slowed and almost stopped, wing tips moving faintly, gathering strength for another rush.

The man had heard the tremendous slap of the great mammal's tail and the snorting gasp as it plunged away. He felt the line go slack again, and he raised his dripping face, and he reached for the bottom with his feet. He found it, but now the water was up to his neck. He plucked at the noose once more with his lacerated hand, but there was no strength in his fingers. He felt the tension come back into the line as the ray began to move again, and for half a second he was tempted to throw himself backward and fight as he had been doing, pitting his strength against the vastly superior strength of the brute.

But the acceptance of imminent death had done something to his brain. It had driven out the fear, and with the fear had gone the panic. He could think now, and he knew with absolute certainty that if he was to make any use of this last chance that had been given him, it would have to be based on the one faculty that had carried man to his preeminence above all beasts, the faculty of reason. Only by using his brain could he possibly survive, and he called on his brain for a solution, and his brain responded. It offered him one.

He did not know whether his body still had the strength to carry out the brain's commands, but he began to swim forward, toward the ray that was still moving hesitantly away from the channel. He swam forward, feeling the rope go slack as he gained on the creature.

Ahead of him he saw the one remaining stake, and he made himself swim faster until he was parallel with the ray and the rope trailed behind both of them in a deep U. He swam with a surge of desperate energy that came from nowhere so that he was slightly in the lead as they came to the stake. He passed on one side of it, the ray was on the other.

Then the man took one last deep breath, and he went down under the black water until he was sitting on the bottom of the bay. He put one foot over the line so that it passed under his bent knee. He drove both his heels into the mud, and he clutched the slimy grass with his bleeding hand, and he waited for the tension to come again.

The ray passed on the other side of the stake, moving faster now. The rope grew taut again, and it began to drag the man back toward the stake. He held his prisoned wrist close to the bottom, under his knee, and he prayed that the stake would not break. He felt the rope vibrate as the barnacles bit into it. He did not know whether the barnacles would cut the rope. All he knew was that in five seconds or less he would be dragged into the stake and cut to ribbons if he tried to hold on; or drowned if he didn't.

He felt himself sliding slowly, and then faster, and suddenly the ray made a great leap forward, and the rope burned around the base of the stake, and the man's foot hit it hard. He kicked himself backward with his remaining strength, and the rope parted, and he was free.

He came slowly to the surface. Thirty feet away the sea devil made one tremendous leap and disappeared into the darkness. The man raised his wrist and looked at the frayed length of rope dangling from it. Twenty inches, perhaps. He lifted his other hand and felt the hot blood start instantly, but he didn't care. He put his hand on the stake above the barnacles and held on to the good rough honest wood. He heard a strange noise, and realized that it was himself, sobbing.

High above, there was a droning sound, and looking up he saw the nightly plane from New Orleans inbound for Tampa. Calm and serene, it sailed, symbol of man's proud mastery over nature. Its lights winked red and green for a moment; then it was gone.

Slowly, painfully, the man began to move through the placid water. He came to the skiff at last and climbed into it. The mullet, still alive, slapped convulsively with its tail. The man reached down with his torn hand, picked up the mullet, let it go.

He began to work on the slipknot doggedly with his teeth. His mind was almost a blank, but not quite. He knew one thing. He knew he would do no more casting alone at night. Not in the dark of the moon. No, not he.

III

Why does a storyteller tell a story? Lots of secondary reasons, I think. To entertain. To inform. To reach out to other people. To release an emotion. To share a conviction. To be the center of attention (that's what you are, momentarily, when you hold an audience). To solve a problem (sometimes I think a good story is nothing but a problem in search of a solution). To pay the grocer or the dentist or the rent. All these things.

But the basic underlying motive probably comes from a kind of impatience, a sort of restless dissatisfaction with the way things actually are. A factual reporter is content to describe his surroundings just as he sees them. But a storyteller isn't. If life doesn't offer enough excitement or romance, he will try to rearrange it until it does. If his surroundings don't appeal to him, he will escape into some imaginary ones that do. If some particular mood is haunting him, he will try to create that mood on paper and lure his readers into it.

Speaking of mood, it's very important. Ideally you should

establish it in the first few lines or paragraphs and then stick to it. Aristotle wrote about the importance in drama of the three unities: unity of place, unity of time, unity of action. He didn't mention mood. Perhaps he should have, because it's usually fatal to try to combine different moods in a short story. If the mood is danger or tension, it should be that throughout. If comedy, likewise. In a stage play perhaps you can throw in a laugh to break the tension in a dramatic scene, but if you do it in a short story, you're likely to spoil the whole thing.

Here's a story where the mood is very gentle, very sentimental, very romantic. All the way through.

A Shining Thing

They sat together on the porch steps, so close that their moon shadow was a single wedge of blackness against the weathered wood. Tomorrow was the wedding, with all the excitement and confusion, tears and laughter. There would be no privacy then. But this quiet hour was their own.

She said, "It's peaceful, isn't it?" She was watching the great stately clouds march over their heads and drop from sight into the quicksilver sea. He was watching her and thought he had never seen her so beautiful.

The wind blew; the waves made little hush-hush sounds, sighing against the sand. "You know," she said, "I always wondered how I'd feel the night before my wedding. Scared, or thrilled, or uncertain, or what."

"You're not scared, are you?"

"Oh, no," she said quickly. She hugged his arm and put her face against his shoulder in the impulsive way she had. "Just a little solemn, maybe. Solemn and gay, and young and old, and happy and sad. Do you know what I mean?"

"Yes," he said. "I know."

"It's love that does it, I suppose," she said. "That old thing. We've never talked about it much, have we? About love itself, I mean."

He smiled a little. "We never had to."

"I'd sort of like to—now," she said. "Do you mind? I'd like to try to tell you how I feel, before tomorrow—happens."

"Will it be any different after tomorrow?"

"No, but I may not be able to talk about it then. It may go down somewhere deep inside, below the talking level."

"All right," he said. "Tell me about love."

She watched a cloud ravel itself against the moon. "Well," she said, "to me it's a shining thing, like a golden fire or a silver mist. It comes very quietly; you can't command it, but you can't deny it, either. When it does come, you can't quite see it or touch it, but you can feel it—inside of you and around you and the person you love. It changes you; it changes everything. Colors are brighter, music is sweeter, funny things are funnier. Ordinary speech won't do—you grope for better ways to express how you feel. You read poetry. Maybe you even try to write it . . ."

She leaned back, clasping her hands around her knees, the moonlight bright and ecstatic on her face.

"Oh, it's so many little things! Waltzing in the dark; waiting for the phone to ring; opening the box of flowers. It's holding hands in a movie; it's humming a sad little tune; it's walking in the rain; it's riding in a convertible with the wind in your hair. It's the quarreling and making up again. It's that first warm, drowsy thought in the morning and the last kiss at night . . ."

She broke off suddenly and gave him a desolate look. "But it's all been said before, hasn't it?"

"Even if it has," he told her gently, "that doesn't make it any less true."

"Maybe I'm just being silly," she said doubtfully. "Is that the way love seems to you?"

He did not answer for a while. At last he said, "I might add a little to your definition."

"You mean, you wouldn't change it?"

"No. Just add to it."

She put her chin in her hands. "Go ahead. I'm listening."

He took out the pipe she had given him and rubbed the smooth grain along his cheek. "You said it was a lot of little things. You're right. I could mention a few that don't have much glitter. But they have an importance that grows . . ."

She watched his lean fingers begin to load the pipe. "Give me some examples," she said.

"Oh, coming home to somebody when day is ended—or waiting for somebody to come home to you. Giving, or getting, a word of praise when none is really deserved. Sharing a joke that nobody else understands. Planting a tree together and watching it grow. Sitting up with a sick child. Remembering anniversaries—do I make it sound terribly dull?"

She did not say anything; she shook her head.

"Everything you mentioned is part of it," he went on, "but it's not all triumphant, you know. It's also sharing disappointment and sorrow. It's going out to slay the dragon, and finding the dragon too much for you, and running away—but going out again the next day. It's the little chips of tolerance that you finally knock off the granite of your own ego: not saying 'I told you so,' not noticing the dented fender in the family car. It's the gradual acceptance of limitations—your own as well as others'. It's discarding some of the ambitions you had for yourself, and planting them in your children . . ." His voice trailed off into the listening night.

"Are you talking," she asked finally, "about living, or loving?"

"You'll find there's not much of one without the other."

"When—when did you learn that?"

"Quite a while ago. Before your mother died." His hands touched her shining hair. "Better go to bed now, baby. Tomorrow's your big day."

She clung to him suddenly. "Oh, Daddy, I'm going to miss you so!"

"Nonsense," he said. "I'll be seeing you all the time. Run along now."

But after she was gone, he sat there for a long time, alone in the moonlight.

IV

One summer when we were staying at our beach cottage, word came that the wife of a friend of ours had been killed in a plane crash. It was a tragic thing; I was haunted by it. *What if such a blow had fallen upon me*, I asked myself; *how would I react? How, indeed, would I survive?*

If you're a storyteller, answers to such questions begin to form in the back of your mind, answers that clamor more and more insistently to be put into words. And the time finally comes when you know you have to try.

One approach is to project yourself into the basic situation and write the story in the first person, as if it were actually happening to you. This way you can use your own emotions and reactions, and since you're feeling them rather than inventing them, they are likely to be believable. If, in addition, you set the story in the actual surroundings you know best, the sense of immediacy is strengthened even further because the setting is completely real.

Sometimes, if you do all this with honesty and intensity,

the story you are bringing to life becomes more real to you than reality itself. A strange and wonderful feeling. While it lasts.

The Return

All through that endless winter I wasn't much good to anyone. I just kept working day and night. And the work I did was competent enough. But when summer came, I went back to the beach.

There were friends who tried to tell me that this was a mistake. Too many memories, they said, too many associations. Too lonely, too this, too that. But I didn't listen to them. Truth was, something kept telling me that I might feel closer to Laura at the cottage than anywhere else. That was all I wanted, really—to be close to her again. This didn't seem unreasonable to me, or morbid. When you've been married to a beautiful girl for five years and death takes her suddenly, like a candle flame blown out by the wind, what are you supposed to do—try to forget her?

So I went back. I told Jim Neville, my law partner, that I would be taking some time off. I would fish, I said, and swim and lie in the sun. Jim didn't try to dissuade me. "Ask me down," he said, "if the channel bass start running. Or even if they don't."

"The first guest," I promised him, "will be you."

He looked at me thoughtfully. He knew an evasion when he heard one. "What about my going with you to open up the place?"

I shook my head. "Thanks, Jim. It'll be all right."

The beach was twenty miles away, across a network of marshes and rivers. I had been at the cottage, alone, when the thing happened. Laura had decided to fly up to see her mother over Labor Day. I didn't go, because I was finishing an important brief. The plane lost a wing in a thunderstorm near Baltimore. The plane lost a wing, and I lost everything. I lost Laura.

That September night, when the call came through, I shut the door of the cottage and locked it and went back to the city. Now, ten months later when I unlocked it again, everything was the same. The book I had been reading was face down near the phone. The cast net I had intended to mend was hanging from a hook. Laura's sunglasses with one earpiece missing still were on the bookcase. Her straw hat with the scarf threaded through it perched on top of a lamp. Some of her face powder still dusted the glass top of her dressing table.

I was prepared for this, braced for it. I had a whole list of things to do. Sweep out the film of sand that had filtered under the doors during the winter storms. Wash the salt off the windows. Clean out the icebox. Check the surf-casting gear, change the lines, oil the reels. Keep busy. Keep occupied. Don't think.

It was late afternoon when I arrived; I knew without looking that the tide was going out. It's strange, but something in me seems to follow the tides, some dim, uncanny instinct. There must be some explanation. All life came out of the sea, didn't it? The cells of our bodies still are bathed in saline solution; perhaps they can feel the slow, insistent tug of the moon. Or perhaps, more simply, if you love the sea enough, your ear can tell the difference in the sound of the surf. Anyway I knew.

The cottage crouched there in the dunes, not fifty feet above high-water mark. We had built it too close to the sea for safety; even a near miss from a hurricane would be the end of it. But Laura had liked it that way. "Let's have a little danger," she said, "even if we have to arrange it." She liked flying too.

By the time I finished sweeping out the sand, the sun was almost down. I went out on the balcony and stood there with the broom in my hand. I felt overcontrolled, overcalm, as if I were standing before a locked door that I did not intend to open. And yet I had a feeling that somewhere there was a key.

From left to right, now, the pelicans were slanting across the burnished water. Night after night Laura and I had sat and watched that twilight parade, saying nothing or very little, the southeast wind coming to us gently, spiced with the faint sweet scent of oleander. Sometimes we'd sit until the moon came up, orange and enormous at first, half-hidden by cloud rack, then a silver coin spinning across the dark floor of heaven, drawing a trail of splintered diamonds across the restless sea.

Nothing had changed. The same wind still blew. Off to the south, across the little river, the islands lay deserted, mile after mile of tangled jungle and empty beaches. A hundred yards to the north, lights were beginning to glow in the Blanchards' cottage. They were a pleasant young couple with two or three small children. Molly Blanchard was a pretty redhead; she and Laura had been good friends. Ted Blanchard, an architect, commuted every day to the city. I liked them both, but somehow I found myself hoping that they would not notice that I had come back.

I stood there while the daylight faded. Finally I brought a folding chair and put it on the balcony. And then I did what I suppose was a foolish thing. I brought another one and put it beside the first. I sat down, and after a while I made a discovery. It was that if I closed my eyes and kept them closed, I no longer felt alone.

It was not simply that I could imagine Laura in the other chair. It was stronger than that. It was as if I somehow could *recall* her—not in the ordinary sense of remembering, but in the sense of summoning her back, back from some blank and misty nowhere into a kind of half-reality that was strange and inexplicable and a little terrifying, but also unbearably sweet. As long as I kept my eyes shut, I could see her—I could *see* her sitting there in the other chair, leaning forward, sun-browned shoulders hunched a little, profile clear and calm against the darkening sky. And while there was no sound except the whisper of the wind and the murmur of the sea, I had the feeling that if I could just listen more intently, I would hear her voice, or the creak of the chair as she leaned back in it, or the faint, far-off echo of her laugh.

Suddenly the telephone rang in the cottage, and instantly I was alone again on a shadowy balcony with an empty chair beside me, facing the empty sea. I stood up, feeling a spark of anger lance through me at this interruption. I went inside and picked up the shrilling instrument. "Yes?"

"Mark?" It was Molly Blanchard's voice, a little uncertain, embarrassed. "Just thought I'd call up to—to say hello and that we're glad you're back."

"Thanks, Molly," I said. "How'd you know?"

"Ted saw Jim Neville in town today. He said you were coming. Look, Mark, why don't you walk over and have some supper with us? My sister's down for her vacation. Maybe we could play some bridge, or just sit around and—"

"Thanks, Molly," I said again, "but I have a million things to do. Give me a rain check, will you?"

"Tomorrow night, maybe?"

"Maybe." I knew she was just trying to be kind. "I'll call you, Molly. Say hello to Ted for me."

I slipped the phone back into its cradle. Outside, now, it was almost dark. Through the window I could see the lights of the Blanchard house, but felt no impulse to leave the cottage—none at all. I told myself that it was because I didn't want to have to make small talk with a stranger. All I knew about Molly's sister was that she was a schoolteacher in another part of the state. But that was not the real reason. The real reason was that I wanted that queer feeling of almost contact with Laura to come back.

It did not come again that night. I turned on the lights, fixed myself some supper, and did some of the things I had planned to do. The loneliness was there, the dull, aching sense of loss, but I was used to that. Ten months is a long time. To combat it, I had devised little stratagems. If I was in one room, I would pretend that Laura was in another, not far away, out of sight, but within call if I should need her. Foolish, of course, but there was comfort in it. Most of the time, if you stop to think about it, what we believe is what we want to believe.

About midnight I took a sleeping pill and went to bed and went to sleep. But I woke suddenly at dawn. All around me was the hush that comes just at the turn of the tide. I must have been dreaming, because I had the distinct impression that someone had been calling me. I got up and went out on the balcony. The air was soft and misty and silver; the planking and the railings were wet with dew. In the East was the first faint smear of crimson. The beach lay vast and empty, the damp sand broken by a series of lagoons left by the receding tide. In one of them I saw a splash as a mullet jumped. Nothing else moved; it was too early even for the pelicans.

I went back into the cottage, put on some swimming trunks, took the cast net from the hook where it was hanging. In past summers Laura and I had often gone casting for mullet in the tidal lagoons. Sometimes she would bring her own net; sometimes she would act as spotter for me. "There's one!" she'd say, pointing at the faint swirl in the water. And the big net would shoot forward and flare into a circle and fall with a crash. You had to be quick and graceful with a cast net—and sharp-eyed. Laura was all three.

Now, with the warm water swirling around my knees, it was easy to imagine that she was behind me, her voice quick with excitement ("Mark! Over there!"), her squeak of mock terror and dismay when she stepped—or thought she stepped—on a crab. As the light grew stronger, so did this impression, until something in me was half-convinced that she *was* there . . . so close, so very close.

But when finally I went back to the cottage with the dripping net, only one set of footprints marked the tawny sand— my own.

It was later that morning that I found the diary. I was clearing out the bureau, putting Laura's things in a box, to be sorted out later or given away. Very steady, very calm, I was braced for this too. And among them was a little pocket diary, an appointment book, really, with four or five lines for each day and notations in Laura's quick, impatient hand. Nothing very significant—usually one-line entries, or sometimes none at all. I leafed through it until I came to the date exactly a year ago, and my hands grew very still.

July 9: Went casting for mullet at sunrise with my own true love. Surf fishing in afternoon.

One year ago to the day. Coincidence? Of course. What else? And yet, why had I wakened so early? What had impelled me to take the net, walk out into the pearly light exactly as we had done a year ago? No wonder I had felt close to Laura. I had been duplicating every move.

I remembered the surf fishing that day, too, on one of the lonely beaches to the south. I had taken three weeks off in July. We had fished almost every day, trying one place after another, taking lunch sometimes and eating it in the shade of scrub oak or palmetto. Or perched on top of a dune, watching the great rollers come creaming in, stately and slow. Swimming when we felt like it, letting the sun dry the brine on our bodies until they were salty to taste or dusty to touch. No one there but ourselves. No other life but the birds and now and then the gleaming black back of a porpoise or sometimes the scuff marks of a great sea turtle's crawl along the sand.

Now this is not going to be easy to put into words, but I must try. As I stood there with the diary in my hands, the idea came to me that perhaps time was not merely horizontal, as I had always thought, like an endless tape unwinding or a river flowing past. The thought came that it might rather be vertical, with each successive moment placed on top of the last, concealing it but not annihilating it so that these concealed moments continued to exist, underneath a layer of time and beyond the reach of ordinary perceptions, but still *there* if only one could brush aside the veil.

The thought also came that if anything could penetrate the veil it would be the sort of love that we had had—Laura and I. I found myself remembering the strange feeling of almost contact on the balcony the night before and again in the lagoon at dawn. And something seemed to whisper that if I just kept on doing the things we had done together, I might somehow break through, even for a moment, and meet her once more—meet her halfway, perhaps, because she might be trying to get through to me too.

This idea did not seem fanciful or ridiculous; it was completely real, perhaps because I wanted to believe it so much. It seemed to me that if we could relive just one moment together—any moment—then I could go on indefinitely alone. You see, when you lose someone so unexpectedly, you think of all the moments that you took for granted, that you didn't appreciate, that you let slide through your fingers like grains of worthless sand. You will do anything, try anything, to get one of them back.

So I tried. That afternoon I took the surf-casting gear and crossed the little river—you could wade it at anything less than high tide—and walked far down the sunlit beach to a place where the tides had carved a series of shallow bays running back into the dunes. On the points of land between these bays the diagonal seas broke with a sound like smothered thunder, and it was in this surf that the game fish swam when wind and tide were right. But it was not fish that I was after now. I was after something far more elusive. I wanted to see if I could find a fragment of the past and make it real again— more real than the present. And something inside me kept whispering that perhaps I could.

In that area of dunes and bays there were half a dozen points that offered promising white water, and I planned to fish one of these each day on the first of the flood tide. That was what Laura and I had done the year before, standing knee-deep or waist-deep in the seething water, the long rods flicking the hooks and lead forty yards or more. I would take the first point and move on down the beach until I came to the last one, where the wreck of an old shrimp boat lay half buried at the foot of the dunes. That was what we had done a year ago. The diary showed it plainly and, anyway, I could remember.

I could remember it far more vividly than anything that had happened since. I could see the sunlight on her hair and the spray on her sunglasses and the way she'd look up at the gulls overhead. I remembered how she fled in panic from a harmless sand shark. I remembered how she lay in the shade of the old wreck and almost went to sleep. I could even remember fragments of dialogue. "The man was right," she said drowsily, "who said that salt water was a cure for everything."

"In one of three forms," I reminded her. "Tears, sweat, or the sea."

"You can have the tears and the sweat," she said. "I'll settle for the sea."

I knew that if I found her anywhere, it would be near this same glittering, fathomless sea.

That afternoon I fished the first two hours of the flood tide. I released the fish I caught; I had no desire to add to the death in the world.

All the time I kept listening, waiting. But there was nothing, no sound, no sign. I was not discouraged by this. I did not expect it to be quick or easy. I knew the mood and timing would have to be exactly right, like the tuning of some infinitely sensitive radar.

Twice there were man-made interruptions. Once a light plane flew low along the beach, dipping its wings in friendly salute. An hour later it droned back. The pilot waved, and the thought came to me that even such a minor distraction as this might somehow interfere, as the telephone call the night before had shattered the strange sense of closeness on the balcony. And so I decided to avoid all such contacts, if I could.

Twice that night, back at the cottage, the telephone rang—perhaps Molly Blanchard, perhaps Jim Neville calling. Both times I ignored it. I decided to fish the early-morning instead of the afternoon tides. There was less chance of seeing or meeting anyone. The less involved I was with the present, the more chance I had of making contact with the past. It seemed as simple to me as that.

Each day, then, I crossed the little river, withdrew into my private world of salt and sand, sun and silence. Each day I felt the remoteness wrap itself more stealthily around me, until I myself became an impersonal, waiting thing—patient as driftwood, lonely as a sea gull's cry. Each morning the tide was an hour later. Each morning I moved to a point farther down the beach. Each morning I felt more removed from reality and closer to—to something.

It was on the fourth morning that I found the writing on the sand.

It came as a shock, unexpected as a blow in the face. I was walking south along the beach, the sun already up, my shadow slanting off along the sand. I had almost reached the point where I intended to fish—and wait and hope—when I saw them. Ten words, written on the damp sand:

How do I love thee? Let me count the ways.

I stood still, staring at the words. For a second—or an eternity—I was convinced that it was a message from Laura. She had known this sonnet, loved it. Surely, then, this was it; this was the breakthrough. Surely these words were from her to me.

But it was all too real. The writing was crisp and fresh. It was below the last high-water mark, so it had been written very recently. A fragment of shell that the writer had used still lay there. There were faint traces of footprints that led down from the soft sand and back again.

I stared down the beach. Nothing. Just the long, shifting lines of surf and the sea wheat stirring on the dunes and a gull circling over the old wreck. I could see no one. But someone had to be there.

I put down my gear and started walking faster. At the base of the next point, where it jutted into the sea, were two more lines:

I have been half in love with easeful Death,
Call'd him soft names in many a mused rhyme.

I began to run then. I knew now where the writer had to be. I also knew that these were no random writings: Browning, Keats, whatever—they were aimed at me. And even as I ran I felt a strange emotion—half anger, half relief, I couldn't tell which.

I came around the prow of the old wreck and stopped. She must have heard me coming, but she did not look up at first. I stared down at her, bracing myself with one hand against the weathered wood. She was about my own age, or a little younger. Her dark hair had red lights in it. When she finally looked up, I saw that she was not beautiful, like Laura, but neither was she plain. Her face had a kind of serenity in it.

"Hello," she said, "I'm Molly's sister, Susan."

Susan. Susan the schoolteacher. She was wearing brown Bermudas and some sort of yellow blouse. A small binocular hung from a strap around her neck. I could see a faint pulse beating at the base of her throat. "You've been looking for her, haven't you?" she said gently. "She's not really here, you know."

I looked over her head, down the long beach, across the world to where the sea met the sky, and I knew she was right. No matter how many ways you love. No matter how close you try to come to easeful death.

"I haven't been spying on you," she said. "Not really. I come out here almost every day to watch the shorebirds. But Molly told me about you. And so . . ." She gave a little shrug.

Still I said nothing. I had the queer conviction that this girl—this woman—already knew how I felt, how I had been feeling. Perhaps she had lived through something like this herself. Perhaps she had learned insight from the poetry she taught. Anyway, she knew.

She pushed back her hair and looked at me. "I think I've had enough for today," she said. "Let's go back, shall we?"

Back to the world, she meant. Back to people. Back to life. Back to living. And still I stood there, not moving, not saying anything. Sometimes it's hard to let go of a dream.

She held out her hand. "Help me up, will you?"

I put out my own and helped her up. Her fingers were light and strong and warm and alive. "Ready?" she asked.

For a moment I didn't reply. I stood there, listening. The world seemed very still, but even as I waited, something changed. Some far-off stirring of the wind, some faintest variation in the sound of the surf. It was like the ghost of a whisper, but I knew what it was. The tide had changed. It was the turn of the tide.

"Yes," I said. "I'm ready. Let's go."

V

No writing is easy. When I hear people say that they just love to write, I regard them with the glum conviction that they're either amateurs or liars. Maybe both. Having written is different. I like that. But to get to that last happy stage you have to pass through the first. There's no other way that I know of.

There are degrees of difficulty, of course. Melodrama—where you write about sea devils and such—is not so bad because it creates its own momentum. It's harder to take little ordinary, everyday occurrences from—say—family living and produce something that will make people smile, or think twice, or even think once.

I used to try this kind of story when the children were small, partly to pay the rent, of course, but partly for propaganda purposes. There seemed to be so much divorce, so much talk of family disintegration, so much downbeat stuff going around that I figured it could do no harm to send out the word occasionally that despite its ordinariness—or maybe because of it—family living could be good-humored and rewarding and fun.

Heaven knows the raw material was all around me in those days. I don't know why I didn't write one of these stories every week.

Well, actually, I do know why. I was too lazy.

Rainy Sunday

"Now this afternoon," said Johnny Trevor, folding his napkin and looking with benevolence at his attentive family, "we will *not* permit the weather, dismal as it is, to get us down. We won't stay cooped up in the apartment either, the way we did last time it rained on Sunday. No, I've decided: We'll do something interesting and educational for a change. Want to know what it is?"

Four pairs of bright eyes regarded him expectantly. They belonged respectively to John Thomas, four; Denny, six; Nancy, eight; and Virginia Trevor who, at twenty-nine, did not look nearly old enough to be the mother of three, but definitely was.

"We'll go," said Johnny Trevor, with the air of an astronomer announcing a new planet, "to the Natural History Museum. I've been meaning to take you for years. It's like the zoo, only better. They have all kinds of animals in their natural settings, just the way they were in real life, and dinosaurs, and a whole whale hanging from the ceiling, and—"

"And the transparent woman!" squealed Nancy, clapping her hands. "We learned about her at school. They've got her in the museum, all made of plastic. You can see her lungs and heart and skeleton—"

"Skeleton?" cried John Thomas in fascination and horror. "You mean she has a *skeleton?*"

"Everybody has a skeleton, dopey," Denny informed him with scorn. "Even you."

"I don't!" replied John Thomas violently. "Do I, Daddy?"

"Well," said his father, "only a small one. Go and change your clothes now. We'll leave soon." He pushed back his chair as the phone shrilled in the living room. "I'll get it. Help your mother clear the table, Nancy."

He came into the kitchen a few minutes later, pulled a dish towel from the rack. "That was Barney."

Virginia handed him a dripping plate. "Anything important?"

"Nope. Wanted me to play handball this afternoon. I told him I had something much better to do."

His wife swished the suds around thoughtfully. "What time did he suggest? Maybe you could . . ."

"No. He has a court reserved for four-thirty, right in the middle of the afternoon. It's all right. He'll be able to pick up a game when he gets there." Johnny stared through the window at the slanting spears of rain. "Those poor old bachelors, I feel sorry for 'em sometimes. Just don't know what to do with themselves."

"We could go to the museum another day, you know."

"And disappoint the children? Certainly not. Besides, I'm looking forward to it!"

Virginia stretched herself on tiptoe and bit the lobe of his ear affectionately. "So am I," she said.

The museum was large and educational, and extremely crowded.

"Now that," said Johnny Trevor, one hand full of rubbers and raincoats, the other restraining John Thomas from climbing over the barrier, "is a family of lions. That's the mother lion over there, see, with her babies. This is the father lion over here. He's very strong and fierce. He really has a pretty good time because the mother lion looks after the cubs. All he has to do is fight with his enemies and bring home things to eat—"

"What things to eat?" cried John Thomas hungrily.

"Oh, antelopes, probably. Or maybe a zebra. Want to go and look at the zebras?"

"I want to look at the dinosaurs, please," Denny said. "They're on the top floor."

"I want to see the transparent lady," Nancy said. "She's down in the basement!"

The museum was well-organized, informative, and huge.

"Now that," said John Trevor, shifting John Thomas to his other shoulder and dropping one rubber in the process, "is a group of cave dwellers. I suppose they were pretty uncomfortable most of the time. But probably they didn't mind. For one thing, they were very tough. They got lots of exercise and kept in shape. They didn't sit at desks the way we do, five days a week. The men went out hunting every day—"

"What did they hunt *with?*" shouted John Thomas, clutching his father's hair.

"With? Oh, spears and knives and things."

"When do we see the whale, Daddy?" asked Denny plaintively.

"I still," said Nancy politely, "would like to see the transparent . . ."

The museum was informative, educational, and *endless.*

"Now *that,*" said Johnny Trevor, "is a rogue elephant. A rogue elephant is one that—well, he's a sort of bachelor elephant. You know, like your Uncle Barney. He has no wife, no children, no nothing. He's miserable, probably. Still, he can go wherever he wants to go, do whatever he wants to . . ."

"Darling," said Virginia, "speaking of Barney, I've been thinking. I know you'd rather be here with us. But maybe you ought to run along and meet him at the club. There's still time, if you hurry."

Her husband gazed at her blankly. "Why, I wouldn't dream of such a thing! What gave you such an idea?"

"Nothing," Virginia said, "except that—well, as you said, he's such a lonely soul. He has so little in his life, and he enjoys those games with you so much. I'll take the kids on home. They're getting tired anyway."

"Well," said Johnny Trevor doubtfully, "if you think I *ought* to go . . ."

"I really do, dear," his wife said. "Poor old Barney. Bring him home for a cold supper, if you want to."

"Maybe I will," said Johnny Trevor happily. He looked at his watch. "Gosh, if I'm going to make it, I'll have to run. Sure you can manage the kids?"

"If a lioness can do it," Virginia assured him, "I can. Go on, now. Run. Shoo!"

She watched her husband's tall figure vanish in the crowd. "Come on, chicks," she said. "We'll see the transparent lady. And the whale. Then I'd better find a delicatessen and drag home a zebra . . . I mean, some potato salad and cold cuts."

Ten mintues later, they emerged from the museum. The rain had stopped; they walked sedately down the glistening steps. "Mummy," said Nancy, "the transparent lady was very interesting. But why didn't they also make a transparent man?"

Virginia Trevor smiled a little. "They didn't have to, dear," she said.

VI

Some years ago I found myself involved, quite unexpectedly, in a curious set of circumstances in Mobile, Alabama.

I still don't know quite what to make of it.

The city fathers had asked me to write a booklet about their town. To lure tourists or new business, I suppose. I was glad to attempt it because Mobile is a charming city, a lot like my hometown, Savannah, only larger. Live oaks and old houses. Spanish moss and camellias. Humid air, soft slurred voices, a thousand church steeples piercing the languid sky.

One afternoon, looking for mood and atmosphere, I walked into one of these churches. At first the cavernous interior seemed dark and deserted. Then, as my eyes became accustomed to the gloom, I noticed someone huddled in one of the back pews not far from where I was standing. The person turned suddenly, and I saw that it was an elderly black man with a halo of white hair, very poorly dressed, almost in rags. When he saw me, he suddenly held out a tattered cap. I was surprised, but there was something urgent, something almost desperate about the gesture, so I fished in my pocket for some silver and dropped it into his cap. Then I wandered about the church, looking at the stained-glass windows, wondering if they deserved mention in the booklet I was planning to write.

As I was about to leave, I heard a strange sound in the stillness. At first I couldn't identify it. But then I realized, with a kind of shock, that it was the old man, weeping. He was hunched forward in the pew, face buried in his hands, shoulders shaking.

Unsure what to do, I went and sat in the pew ahead of him and asked him what the trouble was. His great dark eyes were overflowing with tears. I gave him my handkerchief because clearly he had none. Then he told me that he had come into the city from somewhere in the surrounding country. He had left his home early that day because he had been evicted for nonpayment of rent. He had no money, no relatives, nowhere to go. He had visited this church once, as a young man, and had always remembered it. Now he was hoping that if he waited long enough, one of the priests would find him and help him.

I didn't know where to look for a priest either. But outside, on the porch steps, I found a woman reading the church announcements on the bulletin board. I asked her where the rectory was, and she pointed across the street. So I went back into the church, got the old man, and escorted him to the path that led to the rectory door. I told him to ring the bell. I said I was sure he would be helped. Then I gave him a little more money and hurried away.

As I walked back to the hotel where my wife and I were staying, I put the whole thing out of my mind. Our room was empty; she hadn't returned from lunch yet. I sat down on the bed, my thoughts concentrated entirely on the booklet I was going to write. I took out my notebook to go over my notes.

And suddenly, out of nowhere, came a rush of emotion so unexpected, so powerful, so overwhelming that I was stunned. I felt as if deep inside me great doors had swung open upon another dimension, and through those doors poured a torrent of feeling so intense that I couldn't begin to limit or control it. I felt a great tidal wave of tears surging up in me. It was the only response I could make, and I did burst into tears. I struggled to understand what was happening, but I was caught in an emotional whirlwind that seemed to blow all my defenses away and leave me helpless.

I knew it had something to do with the old black man. I seemed to see his eyes looking at me, full of tears, dark pools that reflected the whole sum of human misery. I saw my own casual efforts to help him and knew a burning sense of shame for their inadequacy. I felt as if all the attempts I had made in the past to help others or oppose evil were feeble things indeed, devoid of any real compassion or caring. The thought seemed to come in a stupendous rush that the true nature of sin lies mainly in what one fails to do—and that in this area, regardless of what we may think, most of us are almost beyond redemption.

I sat there, stricken. In the mirror I could see the tears pouring down my face. Great sobs were caught in my chest. My throat was too tight to let any sound come through.

The door opened, and Pam came in.

What she thought, I don't know, but I'll never forget how she came over and put her arms around me. I knew she must be alarmed—I had never acted like that before (or since)—and so with the small part of my mind that still seemed to be functioning normally I choked out a few words of reassurance. I was all right, I said; at least, I soon would be all right. She just sat there and held me.

Gradually the storm—or whatever it was—subsided. The indescribable sense of grief, of pity, of anguish, of compassion, of a desperate yearning for the inexpressible faded. It faded slowly, though. For months I couldn't think back to those moments in that hotel room without a feeling of tightness in my throat and the sting of tears behind my eyes.

One thing hasn't faded: the conviction that, whatever happened, it was not just some queer internal reaction, some odd psychological backlash. No. It was too strong for that, too sudden. Some invisible finger of tremendous power reached out and touched me. It came from outside.

Looking back, I've often wondered if something in the atmosphere of that church in Mobile, something I was not even aware of at the time, set the stage for the whole episode. Certainly churches of all kinds are centers of spiritual power. Even forlorn, abandoned ones. Down in the Deep South where I live, as you drive along country roads you often see old wooden churches, shutters sagging, belfries askew, no one apparently caring about them or for them. And yet, no matter how decayed, they have a certain dignity, a kind of patience, almost as if they were waiting for someone or some thing to come and restore them to life.

I remember asking myself one time how such a small, forgotten church might be revived. *What if*, I said to myself, *what if it happened like this?*

The Good Things of Life

Near the crest of the hill he felt the rear wheels of the car spin for half a second, and he felt a flash of the unreasonable irritability that had been plaguing him lately. He said, a bit grimly, "Good thing it didn't snow more than an inch or two. We'd be in trouble if it had."

His wife was driving. She often did, so that he could make notes for a sermon or catch up on his endless correspondence by dictating into the tape recorder he had had built into the car. Now she looked out at the woods and fields gleaming in the morning sunlight. "It's pretty, though. And Christmasy. We haven't had a white Christmas like this in years."

He gave her an amused and affectionate glance. "You always see the best side of things, don't you, my love?"

"Well, after hearing you urge umpteen congregations to do precisely that . . ."

Arnold Barclay smiled, and some of the lines of tension and fatigue went out of his face. "Remember the bargain we made twenty years ago? I'd do the preaching and you'd do the practicing."

Her mouth curved faintly. "I remember."

They came to a crossroads, and he found that after all these years he still remembered the sign: LITTLEFIELD, 1 MILE. He said, "How's the time?"

She glanced at the diamond watch on her wrist: his present to her this year. "A little after ten."

He leaned forward and switched on the radio. In a moment his own voice, strong and resonant, filled the car, preaching a Christmas sermon prepared and recorded weeks before. He listened to a sentence or two, then smiled sheepishly and turned it off. "Just wanted to hear how I sounded."

"You sound fine," Mary Barclay said. "You always do."

They passed a farmhouse, the new snow sparkling like diamonds on the roof, the Christmas wreath gay against the front door. "Who lived there?" he asked. "Peterson, wasn't it? No, Johannsen."

"That's right," his wife said. "Eric Johannsen. Remember the night he made you hold the lantern while the calf was born?"

"Do I ever!" He rubbed his forehead wearily. "About this new television proposition, Mary. What do you think? It would be an extra load, I know. But I'd be reaching an enormous audience. The biggest—"

She put her hand on his arm. "Darling, it's Christmas Day. Can't we talk about it later?"

"Why, sure," he said, but something in him was offended all the same. The television proposal was important. Why, in fifteen minutes he would reach ten times as many people as

Saint Paul had reached in a lifetime! He said, "How many people did the Littlefield church hold, Mary? About a hundred, wasn't it?"

"Ninety-six," his wife said. "To be exact."

"Ninety-six!" He gave a rueful laugh. "Quite a change of pace."

It was that, all right. It was years since he had preached in anything but metropolitan churches. The Littlefield parish had been the beginning. Now, on Christmas morning, he was going back. Back for an hour or two, to stand in the little pulpit where he had preached his first hesitant, fumbling sermon twenty years ago.

He let his head fall back against the seat and closed his eyes. The decision to go back had not been his, really; it had been Mary's. She handled all his appointments, screening the innumerable invitations to preach or speak. A month ago she had come to him. There was a request, she said, for him to go back to Littlefield and preach a sermon on Christmas morning.

"Littlefield?" he had said, incredulous. "What about that Washington invitation?" He had been asked to preach to a congregation that would, he knew, include senators and cabinet members.

"We haven't answered it yet," she said. "We could drive to Littlefield on Christmas morning, if we got up early enough . . ."

He had stared at her. "You mean, you think we *ought* to go back there?"

She had looked back at him calmly. "That's up to you, Arnold." But he knew what she wanted him to say.

Making such a decision wasn't so hard at the moment, he thought wearily. Not resenting afterward—that was the difficult part. Maybe it wouldn't be so bad. The church would be horribly overcrowded, the congregation would be mostly farmers, but . . .

The car stopped; he opened his eyes.

They were at the church, all right. There it sat by the side of the road, just as it always had—if anything, it looked smaller than he remembered it. Around it the fields stretched away, white and unbroken, to the neighboring farmhouses. But there were no cars, there was no crowd, there was no sign of anyone. The church was shuttered and silent.

He looked at Mary, bewildered. She did not seem surprised. She pushed open the car door. "Let's go inside, shall we? I still have a key."

The church was cold. Standing in the icy gloom, he could see his breath steam in the gray light. He said, and his voice sounded strange, "Where is everybody? You said there was a request . . ."

"There was a request," Mary said. "From me." She moved forward slowly until she was standing by the pulpit. "Arnold," she said, "the finest sermon I ever heard you preach was right here in this church. It was your first Christmas sermon; we hadn't been married long. You didn't know our first baby was on the way—but I did. Maybe that's why I remember so well what you said.

"You said that God had tried every way possible to get through to people. He tried prophets and miracles and revelations—and nothing worked. So then He said, 'I'll send them something they can't fail to understand. I'll send them the simplest and yet the most wonderful thing in all My creation. I'll send them a Baby . . .' Do you remember that?"

He nodded wordlessly.

"Well," she said, "I heard that they had no minister here now, so I knew they wouldn't be having a service this morning. And I thought . . . well, I thought it might be good for . . . for both of us if you could preach that sermon again. Right here, where your ministry began. I just thought . . ."

Her voice trailed off, but he knew what she meant. He knew what she was trying to tell him, although she was too loyal and too kind to say it in words. That he had gotten away from the sources of his strength. That as success had come to him, as his reputation had grown larger, some things in him had grown smaller. The selflessness. The humility. The most important things of all.

He stood there, silent, seeing himself with a terrifying clarity: the pride, the ambition, the hunger for larger and larger audiences. Not for the glory of God. For the glory of Arnold Barclay.

He clenched his fists, feeling panic grip him, a sense of terror and guilt unlike anything he had ever known. Then faintly, underneath the panic, something else stirred. He glanced around the little church. She was right, Mary was right, and perhaps it wasn't too late. Perhaps here, now, he could rededicate himself . . .

Abruptly he stripped off his overcoat, tossed it across the back of a pew. He reached out and took both of Mary's hands. He heard himself laugh, an eager, boyish laugh. "We'll do it! We'll do it just the way we used to! You open the shutters; that was your job, remember? I'll start the furnace. We'll have a Christmas service just for the two of us. I'll preach that sermon, all for you!"

She turned quickly to the nearest window, raised it, began fumbling with the catch that held the shutters. He opened the door that led to the cellar steps. Down in the frigid basement he found the furnace squatting, as black and malevolent as ever. He flung open the iron door. No fire was laid, but along the wall wood was stacked, and kindling, and newspapers.

He began to crumple papers and thrust them into the furnace, heedless of the soot that blackened his fingers. Overhead he heard the sound that made him pause. Mary was trying the wheezy old melodeon. "Ring the bell, too," he shouted up the stairs. "We might as well do the job right!"

He heard her laugh. A moment later, high in the belfry, the bell began to ring. Its tone was as clear and resonant as ever, and the sound brought back a flood of memories: the baptisms, the burials, the Sunday dinners at the old farmhouses, the honesty and brusqueness and simple goodness of the people.

He stood there, listening, until the bell was silent. Then he struck a match and held it to the newspapers. Smoke curled reluctantly. He reached up, adjusted the old damper, tried again. This time a tongue of flame flickered. For perhaps five minutes he watched it, hovering over it, blowing on it. When he was sure that it was kindled, he went back up the cellar steps.

The church was a blaze of sunlight. Where the window glass was clear, millions of dust motes whirled and danced;

where there were panes of stained glass, the rays fell on the old floor in pools of ruby and topaz and amethyst. Mary was standing at the church door. "Arnold," she said, "come here."

He went and stood beside her. After the darkness of the cellar, the sun on the snow was so bright that he couldn't see anything.

"Look," she said in a whisper. "They're coming."

Cupping his hands round his eyes, he stared out across the glistening whiteness, and he saw that she was right. They were coming. Across the fields. Down the roads. Some on foot. Some in cars. They were coming, he knew, not to hear him, not to hear any preacher, however great. They were coming because it was Christmas Day, and this was their church and its bell was calling them. They were coming because they wanted someone to give them the ancient message, to tell them the good news.

He stood there with his arm round his wife's shoulders and the soot black on his face and the overflowing happiness in his heart. "Merry Christmas," he said. "Merry Christmas. And thank you. Thank you, darling."

VII

One summer in Colorado I met a little widow-lady named Tinker. That was what everyone called her. Faded blue eyes with a faraway look. White hair, patient hands. Weighed maybe ninety pounds. She was twice my age—perhaps more—but somehow we became friends, and gradually she told me the story of her life. She didn't think it was remarkable, but I did. It was so American, so heartbreaking, so brave, so *true* that I asked her if I might try to put it into words.

She said she didn't mind, and so I did try. I didn't have to invent anything, except the hospital frame I put around it. The rest was all there, just as she told it. Her love of the mountains impressed me a lot. It reminded me of the way I felt about the sea.

It's not easy to tell a life story in three or four thousand words. You have to cover so much ground that it's likely to lose focus and tension and sound like the synopsis of a novel. But anyway, I tried.

Tinker was thrilled when I sent her the story and told her I thought it would find a home somewhere. When a magazine finally bought it, I sent Tinker half the money. I've regretted that ever since, really.

I should have sent her all of it.

Until the Doctor Comes

"Now just try to rest," Miss Saunders said in the soothing voice she reserved for patients on the critical list. "Just close your eyes and think about the pleasantest things you can. You'll be surprised how fast the time goes until the doctor comes."

She said these things half automatically, forgetting that in this case she really did not have to say them. Some patients begged for their injection ahead of schedule, but Mrs. Benton didn't. She just lay there, waiting.

Miss Saunders moved around the bed, her starched skirt rustling. She turned the lamp aside so that only a faint glow touched the worn hands folded on the immaculate sheet. Then she went down the corridor, her white shoes almost soundless on the rubber-tiled floor. At the reception desk Miss Andersen looked up. "How's she doing?"

"Not too well. But she doesn't complain."

"I know." Miss Andersen looked at the big wall clock. "Dr. Gregg will be here soon."

"That's what I told her," Miss Saunders said.

Old Mrs. Benton had closed her eyes. That was the easiest part of Miss Saunders' instructions. Thinking pleasant thoughts—that was not always possible. Sometimes the black tide of pain came flooding in so fast that you couldn't think. You could only feel.

Tonight the pain was there, of course, but it didn't seem to be moving. That was good because when it kept still you could gauge its strength and set aside certain reserves to take care of it. You could forget it, almost, for a little while.

Think about the pleasantest things, Miss Saunders had said. A nice girl, a kind and patient girl. She worked hard eight hours a day and considered herself overworked, of course. Mrs. Benton smiled a little to herself. Why, when she was that age . . .

But why not try to begin at the beginning? Why not let the scenes march in orderly progression out of the past, the good scenes and the bad ones too, fragmentary as memory pictures always are, but filling the necessary minutes?

Old Mrs. Benton took a deep breath. She had tried it before, this plunge into the past in order to escape the present. Never too successfully. Either she got tired or the pain broke through or one of the nurses came in with some medication. But at least in these previous efforts she had found the best starting point.

Commencement, they called it, appropriately enough. She called for the memory and there it was, sharp and clear behind her eyelids—the hot June night in the little Missouri town, the long white dresses, the flushed eager faces. Her own heart jumping like a cricket when her name was called: "Hester Knowles." Old Professor Lenroot's beard bobbing as he handed out the diplomas. Twenty-three in that graduating class, the best class (they were sure of that) from the best teachers' college west of the Alleghenies.

They liked that word, best. It was the key word in their class motto, taken from Browning—"The best is yet to be." They believed that passionately, every one of them, as they sang their last songs together and cried a little and swore undying devotion.

The best, for Hester, was the telegram that came that summer. It wasted no words. "Latin teacher needed Red Springs, Wyoming. Salary $85." Why, that was fifteen dollars more than any salary available in Missouri! Would she go? Of course she would! Her family needed the money, or part of it. And she had always wanted to see a mountain.

She still remembered the panic that gripped her as the train slowed for the little station, lost on the interminable prairie. She got off hesitantly, the smell of dust and green plush still in her nostrils. She stood there for a moment, small and pretty and frightened, the blue veil that had seemed so gay and grownup in Missouri trailing dejectedly down her back. The train coughed and went away. She followed it longingly with her eyes and suddenly she saw them, rising like God's own decision above the sun-baked plain—the Rockies, purple with distance, crowned with the eternal snows.

She felt her throat tighten; tears came into her eyes. A foot scraped on the gray boards behind her. Turning, she saw a rough-looking man with his hat in his hand. "You the new schoolmarm, Miss?"

She nodded, aware of the sly appraising glances from the idlers around the station but somehow frightened no longer. That was an odd thing. The moment she saw the mountains, all her fears left her. She no longer felt like a stranger. She felt as if she had come home.

That winter went fast. She shared a boardinghouse room with another teacher, Trudy Blackmar. Hester was prettier but Trudy was the lively one. She teased Hester into learning how to dance, something sternly frowned on then in Methodist Missouri. They made divinity fudge on Sunday afternoons and occasionally were escorted to that new marvel in Red Springs, the moving-picture show. There were plenty of eager young men—ranchers, miners, cowboys. But somehow none of them was quite right, none was the dream prince—until Dr. Jim Benton came to town.

She heard of him before she saw him, heard he was tall and slender, with brown hair and blue eyes and a gentle smile. Smooth shaven, too. That was good. She couldn't imagine herself . . . she blushed sometimes at her own thoughts.

They were introduced, eventually, in the drugstore one afternoon. He looked down at her, smiling. "So you're the beautiful Miss Hester Knowles. Why, you're even smaller than they said. But good things . . ."

"Come in small prescriptions," she finished for him rather

tartly and flounced away before he could see how flustered she was.

He came to call the next night. By the end of the week they knew they were in love. It came sweeping down on them like the torrents that roared down the canyons in the spring, an elemental force suddenly released, life-giving and irresistible.

But quiet too. They used to sit on the porch of her boardinghouse, facing the mountains, dreaming their great golden dreams. They would be married and as soon as Jim's health improved—he had come west from Pennsylvania because of a touch of lung sickness—they would somehow go to Europe. Jim would study in Vienna, would become rich and famous. Hester would give up teaching, would devote all her time to studying music. She might become a great pianist, who could tell?

She wrote the fateful letter to her family one night in May with the kerosene lamp turned low and outside the open window all the sweet mysterious scents of spring rising from the purple darkness of the plain. "I must ask you to release me," she wrote, "from my promise to send you money every month. But if you knew Jim, you would understand. He is everything I could ever want in a man. Only two things are lacking—money and perfect health. We can make the one and perhaps God will send us the other. . . ."

Bewildered but loyal, her family consented. They were married in June, the day after school closed. Everybody in Red Springs came to the wedding. Trudy was maid of honor and sobbed desperately, unsure whether she was crying for Hester married or herself unmarried or the awful sense of life fulfilling itself and moving inexorably on.

For two years, then, they struggled to make ends meet. Hester was not unhappy; she had her friends and her new baby. But one night, after reckoning up the amounts owed him—amounts he was too proud or too gentle to press people for—Jim said wearily, "Let's stop fooling ourselves, Hettie. We'll never get anywhere in Red Springs. Why don't we head for the hills? Plenty of land back in there for homesteaders.

We could build our own house, raise our own stock, I could keep on doctoring and with the farm we'd have a double source of income. Why don't we just pull up stakes?"

It wasn't Europe. It certainly wasn't Vienna. But they went. They went west, as millions of Americans had gone before them, each one confident that the best was yet to be.

They came at last to the settlement they had chosen in northern Utah, sixty miles from the nearest railroad. They got a room above a livery stable, the best they could find. The sheets had been used, and there were crawling things that Hester tried not to think about. In the yard there was a trough, and cattle from the field behind the stable kept coming in to drink. Lying there close to Jim, her arm around little James, Hester felt as if she had reached the end of the earth. She never forgot the lonely tinkle of those cowbells or the pale hostile glitter of the stars.

The Homestead Law required them to live on their land for a certain time before they started to build. They bought a sheep wagon, a clumsy canvas-covered descendant of the Conestoga. Under the burning August sun they camped out in a sea of sagebrush, ringed by the silent mountains. The nearest house was five miles away. Once Jim was called to a confinement case and stayed three nights. Hester barricaded the wagon doors, listened to the coyotes howl, and lived in unreasonable terror of bears.

But the bears stayed up in the hills. The highest mountain, to the northwest, was a rich tawny color, like a crouching lion. Hester mentally christened it Old Sorrel and tried to persuade herself that it was her guardian and friend. She used to talk to it aloud sometimes, when Jim was away.

Winter drove them back to the settlement but the next spring they were out again, building a makeshift cabin, clearing the land. There were times when every one of those bare acres seemed as big as the whole state of Utah. Hester tried plowing but she was too light and the plow handles simply tossed her aside. Jim did it all. The palms of his hands blistered at first, then grew tough. Hester had to content herself with pulling sagebrush from the plowed land, stacking it to be burned.

They had plans for a real house, and they worked on that after supper while the long shadows crept down from the hills. By mid-summer the cellar was dug, the walls braced temporarily. There was a makeshift flight of steps, up and down which little James scrambled happily. Until it happened.

There was no warning. Bending over the stove in the cabin, Hester heard her husband's agonized shout, ran with fear snapping at her heels, saw Jim digging frantically at the huge mound of fallen earth that filled one side of the excavation. "The baby!"

Hester hurled herself upon the evil brown clinging stuff, clawed at it with her hands while Jim shoveled, wild-eyed. Once, somewhere underneath, they thought they heard a feeble sound.

"We're coming," cried Hester, the desperate tears blinding her.

They did come, at last, to the limp little body. They wiped the dirt from the calm sweet face; they breathed into the pale mouth; they pumped the tiny unresisting lungs. Long after they knew it was hopeless, they kept trying.

The sun went down as it always did, the stars came out, the indifferent breeze sighed down the canyon. All night long Hester crouched, motionless, beside the cot. Nothing Jim could say made any difference. *If we hadn't come here, it wouldn't have happened. If we hadn't come to this awful place . . .*

In the cold grayness before dawn, she moved stiffly. On the other side of the cot, Jim had fallen asleep, his face pinched with exhaustion and misery. She went outside. The cellar lay before her like a scar, and then the sagebrush, and then the mountains. She looked up at the tallest of them. *You let it happen*, she said inside herself. Her eyes were hot and dry; the only emotion she felt was hatred.

The sky changed; it lost its somber look, became a pure bottomless blue. Light flashed from the crest of Old Sorrel as it caught the first spear hurled by the onrushing sun. The valley still lay in darkness but the golden flood poured down the heights like an avalanche, driving the shadows back. As she watched, hating it all, a phrase came unbidden into Hester's mind: "God is mindful of His own. . . ."

Something seemed to burst inside of her then and she flung her apron over her head, and wept.

Outside in the hospital corridor, light footsteps approached. Old Mrs. Benton tensed herself uneasily. Not because of the pain. It was just that she had never done so well with her remembering; she did not want to be interrupted now. Nor was she. The footsteps went past her door, receded, died away. . . .

In the end they didn't leave the homestead, although they talked about it. They stayed and put their mark upon the land, and the land in turn left its mark upon them. The settlement grew from a collection of weather-beaten shacks to a small town, but Hester seldom went there. She was ashamed in a way of her old clothes and leathery skin.

Other babies were born—first Jeremy, then the twins, finally little Charity. When they were small, Hester would take them into the fields with a box of broken toys, let them play while she pulled the interminable sagebrush.

Somehow the double income never materialized. Or if it did, it vanished twice as fast. Jim went on with his doctoring. Sometimes he rode thirty-five miles to make a call, fording the icy streams. Often he was paid in provisions—a sack of potatoes, a couple of chickens, a piece of salt pork. Sometimes he wasn't paid for months; sometimes not at all. They used to laugh when a sheepish farmer would ride up and settle the bill for his wife's last confinement. It usually meant another stork party was brewing in that household.

Sometimes, when Jeremy was old enough to watch the smaller children, Hester would go on calls with Jim. She learned to drop the chloroform carefully onto the gauze mask when labor was difficult or instruments had to be used. She grew nervous, sometimes, but never once, out of all the women he delivered did Jim lose a baby or a mother.

"I declare, Hettie," said sharp-eyed Lydia Combs at the crossroads store one day, "if I was married to that doctor of your'n, I'd worry aplenty about him stayin' away days at a time, seein' all those women."

"If I was married to your husband," said Hester serenely, "I guess I'd worry too!"

She had a rival, though. It was the telephone. When they first had it, she was overjoyed at the thought that she could talk to Jim across the lonely miles or at least pick up the receiver and hear friendly voices. But she learned to hate it. Folks who had to ride half a dozen miles to get the doctor came only in a real emergency. But when they could summon him just by turning a crank . . .

There was that dreadful night—early April, it was—when Jim was sick in bed with a fever of 102. The weather was horrible, a mountain mixture of sleet and hail, and the phone rang: two long, three short. It was Jed Digbee, the surly farmer who had played them a dirty trick the year before. He'd been diverting more than his own share of water from the main irrigation ditch. So to remove suspicion from himself, he'd accused the Bentons of the same thing. But now his child was sick with a flaming sore throat, and he wanted a doctor to come right away.

"He can't come," said the doctor's wife. "He's in bed with a fever himself."

"He'd better come!" yelled Digbee."I ain't goin' to listen to no excuses. He better get over here right away . . ."

She hung up on the rest of the tirade.

"Who was that?" Jim asked from the bedroom.

She told him, while the phone shrilled again and again. "But you're not going anywhere."

He lay there for quite a while thinking. Finally he sat up and reached for his clothes. "I've got to go. Could be diphtheria."

"Jim," she said. "Jim, please! Don't you ever think about yourself? Don't you ever think about *us?*"

"Sure," he said. "Sure I do."

He was down at the barn, saddling up, when she heard the thunder of hoofs, and the door burst open and there was Digbee, red eyed, with a six-gun in his hand. "That husband of yours is comin' with me," he told her, "or I'll kill him right here and now!"

She could still remember the white-hot flash of fury that roared through her and with it the knowledge that if there was any killing to be done, she would do it. But all she said to him was, "He's already gone to your child, Mr. Digbee."

They never settled that bill, either. . . .

They had some good times, though. Now and then Jim would take a notion to go on a camping trip in the hills. He loved to fish and, if no babies were due, off they'd go in the double buggy with Kit and Doll, the two old mares, twitching their ears as if they disapproved of the whole thing. It was hard to blame them, really. The roads were nothing but boulder-strewn trails. But they drove on, the baby in Hester's lap, the twins and Jeremy jouncing beside her, until at last they reached their campsite, the mountain lake where the aspen quivered and the great peaks studied their reflections in the quiet water.

Year after year they fought their unending war against hail and hardship, drought and disease. And one autumn, after a summer full of disasters, Jim said, "We've got to try something else, Hettie. Milk and butter—that's the thing. If we had a small herd of Holsteins . . ."

"And what," said Hester, thinking of the ruined crops, "would you suggest using for money?"

Jim's face looked sharp and somehow desperate. "We'll have to mortgage the farm." Then he smiled at her. "Things'll get better. You'll see."

They did it. They bought the cows. And a bull. They got a hired man to tend them, but he was shiftless, lazy, no-account. If Hester had worked before, now she slaved. Milking, helping reluctant calves to be born. Trying to do all the rest of it—the children, the cooking, the washing.

Sometimes, usually when Jim was away, the cows would find a break in the fence, get out, scatter. Many a mile she rode looking for them, reeling in the saddle from plain exhaustion, the slanting rain searching her face with its little cold knives.

Sometimes, just to keep awake, she'd recite what she could remember of the marriage service: "I, Hester . . . thee, James." She'd keep time with old Major's plodding hoofs. "Richer . . . poorer. Sickness . . . health . . . better . . . worse." Lost cows were worse than anything she had bargained for.

And yet there were moments. Resting once, beside Jim's favorite trout stream, she caught him looking at her strangely. "What is it?" she asked.

"All this." He swung his arm wide. "Not much like Vienna, is it?"

She did not answer; she had had little time to think of Vienna.

"Sometimes," he said slowly, "I wonder."

He stared at the rushing water and she knew what he meant. He meant all the dreams discarded, all the hopes put aside, all the aching might-have-beens. He meant the mystery and the hint of meaning at the heart of the mystery. He meant the undecipherable wherefore of everything, the impenetrable why.

He raised his head at last. "But there's one thing I do know: I love you."

So they went on through the treacherous years, the good-hearted years, the years so slow to pass, so quickly gone. Summer and winter, seedtime and harvest, bad times and good. The typhoid epidemic that struck five families almost overnight. The country dances where the young wives brought their babies and laid them in rows among all the blankets.

They went on for twenty years and thought to have twenty more. But one spring, just as her husband was climbing into the car on an emergency call, she cried out, "Jim, there's a tick on you."

He slapped the back of his neck, pulled off the loathsome thing.

"Wait," she said, "let me disinfect it."

"Later." He gunned the engine. "The Morgan child's cut his foot with an ax."

Ten days later, Jim was dead of Rocky Mountain spotted fever.

Hester was like a dazed animal. At first a kind of unbelieving numbness held her, but one evening the loneliness struck her like a blow. She was sitting on the porch in the dark. The children were asleep. It was just the way it always was when Jim was away on a case and might come driving home any minute. But the road stretched away, dark and silent, and suddenly she knew that he wasn't coming, ever again, and she wanted to howl like a coyote or beat her forehead against the floor or maybe get the old shotgun from where it hung above the door and end it for all of them.

She even stood up and took a couple of steps before she hooked her arm around one of the posts that held up the porch roof. She pressed her mouth against the rough wood, but she could not stifle the question that screamed inside of her: *Why? Why has this happened to me? What have I done? What has any of us done?*

There was no answer anywhere, not anywhere in the brooding hills or the arching sky. Only silence and emptiness so big that they were their own answer.

She went back to teaching. It was all she could do. Jeremy was fifteen, and he did as much work as any man, but even so, the mortgaged farm went downhill. They would have lost it if a brother of Jim's, also a doctor, hadn't sent them help now and then. It was a time that didn't bear thinking about.

Somehow, the years went past. Jeremy married, went overseas, came back safely, had two children. The twins worked their way through college, got themselves good city jobs. Charity married a farmer not far down the valley. She worked hard but it wasn't like the old days. Now they had good roads, washing machines, and crop insurance. Hester was glad of it.

She stayed in her house, and all the family came at Thanksgiving and again at Christmas. The grandchildren were always welcome, but it was lonely at times. She found too that she grew tired easily, and deep inside her was the pain that had been there for years now.

She went to a doctor at last and he looked at her gravely. "Your husband was a physician, Mrs. Benton. You should have known enough to come to me sooner."

I did know enough, thought Hester with a secret smile. *But I didn't want to come any sooner. You might have cured me.*

She wasn't old, really, but she felt as if she had lived a million years. She was glad when they brought her to the hospital. She said to herself, *I've earned some rest.*

So there it all was, behind her now, good and bad, joy and sorrow, pleasure and pain, the great opposites which drew their meaning only from each other. There it all was.

How did I do it? she asked herself. *What kept me going sometimes, why didn't I just give up?*

She remembered, then, the way the sunlight touched Old

Sorrel the morning after little James died, and she knew what had kept her going. Not duty, not courage, not even instinct. It was hope. It was the unshakable conviction that somehow, sometime, no matter what, the best was yet to be. And she knew, although she was dying, she was hoping still.

Her mind was very clear now, and she saw that it was mankind's greatest gift and glory, this refusal to stop hoping. She saw too that it could not be illusion because if it were, life would be a clumsy joke, stupid and pointless and devoid of meaning.

Her eyelids flickered as the mountain of pain inside her shifted suddenly. It shifted and eased itself down and came to rest again. But it was different, somehow; everything was different. She did not try to open her eyes but her lips moved. "Jim," she said, "Jim!"

Noiseless, now, on rubber-shod feet the nurse and intern came down the corridor. But they were too late. The doctor— her doctor—had already come for Hester Benton.

VIII

The closest I ever came to being a tycoon, I think, was when I was eleven and used to sell crabs. My friend Anderson Hammond, who was Huck Finn to my Tom Sawyer, and I used to catch a bushel or so, boil them in a large black pot over a charcoal fire, put them in a rusty red wagon and drag them around the island selling them for twenty-five cents a dozen.

Catching the crabs, I must say, was more fun than boiling them. More fun for the crabs, too, I imagine. You could catch them with hand lines and a scoop net; that was the easiest way. Or, if you were in a pensive mood, you could lower crab baskets from an old gray dock and think deep thoughts while you waited for the crabs to find the bait. Old leg-of-lamb bones from Sunday dinner were good bait if you could wheedle them away from the cook. So were frogs, if you squashed them up a bit. Dead sharks were no good; the crabs didn't like them, and I didn't blame them.

We found one remarkable place on a marshy sandbar

where, at a certain tide, you could tramp through the marsh grass yelling and howling and beating the grass with sticks, which so annoyed the crabs—who after all had gone there with romantic expectations looking for mates—that they would skitter angrily across the shallows headed for deep water. All you had to do was intercept them.

This led to such sudden opulence that we hardly knew what to do with all the quarters. Usually we'd take them down to a palace of vice near the old pavilion where you could play poker by rolling rubber balls into holes marked with playing cards, kings and queens and jacks and so on. You got a coupon if you rolled a good hand. I finally had so many coupons that I redeemed them for a stupendous tea set with about a hundred and ninety pieces of hideous china made in Japan. I gave it to my mother, who smiled bravely and said she loved it. A true lady. I think she knew it represented most of my profits for the summer.

The reason I'm telling you all this is that in the next story I appear as a delivery boy for a florist's shop. If you must know, I never did work in a florist's shop. I was too busy catching crabs.

A Rose for Miss Caroline

Every Saturday night, all through that lazy spring, I used to take a rose to Miss Caroline Wellford. Every Saturday, rain or shine, at exactly eight o'clock.

It was always the best rose in the shop. I would watch Old Man Olsen nest it tenderly in green tissue paper and fern. Then I would take the narrow box and pedal furiously through the quiet streets and deliver the rose to Miss Caroline.

In those days, after school and on Saturdays, I worked as delivery boy for Olsen the florist. The job paid only three dollars a week, but that was a lot of pocket money for a teenager then, and I used to squander it gloriously. My mother always wanted to make me save some of it, but my father said no. He said there were only a few years in your life when you could spend money on yourself without your conscience hurting you, and I had better make the most of them.

From the beginning there was something a little strange about those roses—or rather, about the circumstances under which I delivered them to Miss Caroline. The night the first one was sent I pointed out to Mr. Olsen that he had forgotten the card.

He peered at me through his glasses like a benevolent gnome. "There isn't any card, James." He never called me Jimmy. "And furthermore the—ah—party sending this flower wants it done as quietly as possible. So keep it under your hat, will you?"

Even then I was old enough to know that the surest way to spoil a secret is to tell it, so I was willing to keep it under my hat. I was glad Miss Caroline was getting a flower, because we all felt sorry for her. As everybody in our small town knew, the worst of all fates had befallen Miss Caroline. She had been jilted.

For years she had been in love with—as good as engaged to—Jeffrey Penniman, one of the ablest young bachelors in town. Keeping herself usefully busy, she had waited while he got himself through medical school. She was still waiting when, halfway through his internship, Dr. Penniman fell in love with a younger, prettier girl and married her.

It was almost a scandal. My mother said that all men were brutes and that Jeffrey Penniman deserved to be horsewhipped. My father said, on the contrary, that it was the right—no, the sacred duty—of every man to marry the prettiest girl who would have him. That's what he had done, my father said, and he hadn't regretted it yet. My mother found it difficult to reply to that.

The girl Jeffrey Penniman married was a beauty, all right. Her name was Christine Marlowe, and she came from a big city, and she looked it. She must have had an uncomfortable time in our town, because naturally the women despised her and said all sorts of unkind things about her.

As for poor Miss Caroline, the effect on her was disastrous. She shut herself in her house, stopped leading her Girl Scout troop, gave up all civic activities. She even refused to play the organ at church any more.

For six months, now, she had been acting like this. She wasn't old, really, or unhandsome, but she seemed determined to turn herself into an eccentric old maid. She looked like a ghost that night when she came to the door. "Hello, Jimmy," she said listlessly. When I handed her the box, she looked startled—, "For me?"

I was inclined to share her incredulity. The notion that Miss Caroline might have a secret admirer lurking somewhere struck me as highly improbable. But all I said was, "Sign here, please."

Again the next Saturday, at exactly the same time, I found myself delivering another rose to Miss Caroline. And the next Saturday yet another. The third time she opened the door so quickly that I knew she must have been waiting. There was a little color in her cheeks, now, and her hair no longer looked so straggly.

The morning after my fourth trip to her house, Miss Caroline played the organ again in church. The rose, I saw, was pinned to her blouse. She held her head high; she did not glance once at the pew where Dr. Penniman sat with his beautiful bride. What courage, my mother said, what character!

Week after week I delivered the rose, and gradually Miss Caroline resumed her normal life. There was something proud about her now, something defiant almost—the attitude of a woman who may have suffered an outward defeat, but who knows inwardly that she is still cherished and loved.

The night came, eventually, when I made my final trip to Miss Caroline's house. I said, as I handed her the box, "This is the last time I'll bring this, Miss Caroline. We're moving away next week. But Mr. Olsen says he'll keep sending the flowers."

She hesitated, then she said, "Come in for a minute, Jimmy."

She led me into her prim sitting room. From the mantel she took a model of a sailing ship, exquisitely carved. "This was my grandfather's," she said. "I'd like you to have it. You've brought me great happiness, Jimmy—you and your roses."

She opened the box, touched the delicate petals. "They say so much, although they are silent. They speak to me of other Saturday nights, happy ones. They tell me that he, too, is lonely . . ." She bit her lip, as if she had said too much. "You'd better go, now, Jimmy. Go!"

Clutching my ship model, I fled to my bicycle. Back at the shop, I did what I had never had the nerve to do. I looked in the file where Mr. Olsen kept his untidy records. I looked under "P" and I found what I was looking for. "Penniman," it said, in Mr. Olsen's crabbed script. "Fifty-two American Beauties—25¢. Total: $13. Paid in advance."

Well, I thought to myself. *Well!*

The years went by, and one day I came again to Olsen's flower shop. I went in. Nothing had changed. Old Man Olsen was making a corsage of gardenias, just as he used to do.

We talked awhile, my old boss and I. Then I said, "Whatever became of Miss Caroline, Mr. Olsen? You remember—she got the roses."

"Miss Caroline?" He nodded. "Why, she married George Halsey—owns the drugstore. Fine fellow. They have two sets of twins."

"Oh!" I said, a bit surprised. Then I decided to show Mr. Olsen how smart I had been. "D'you suppose," I said, "that Mrs. Penniman ever knew her husband was sending flowers to his old flame?"

Mr. Olsen sighed. "James," he said, "you never were very bright. Jeffrey Penniman didn't send them. He never even knew about 'em."

I stared at him. "Who did, then?"

"A lady," said Mr. Olsen. He put the gardenias carefully into a box. "A lady who said *she* wasn't going to sit around watching Miss Caroline make a martyr of herself at *her* expense. Christine Penniman sent those roses.

"Now *there*," said Mr. Olsen, closing the lid with finality, "was a woman for you!"

IX

I've always admired salesmen because I'm such a poor salesman myself. I found that out in college where for a while I tried to be a seller of laundry contracts to other students. I was a dismal failure, because I had a fatal tendency to put myself in the shoes of the prospective customer and feel nothing but annoyance at my uninvited knock on his door. My approach then became, in manner if not actual words, "You don't want this wretched laundry contract, do you? I wouldn't, if I were you!"

Still, even then I knew *somebody* had to sell laundry contracts, and everything else, for that matter. Product excellence isn't enough. Someone has to bring the product to the attention of the consumer, do it cheerfully, do it with sincerity and conviction, and do it without making a nuisance of himself. Courageous people, these salesmen, braving hostility, facing rejection, riding into battle daily, as Arthur Miller said, on nothing but a shoeshine and a smile.

And most of them, basically, are such decent people. Perhaps in this next story I was trying to let them know that I admire them.

And need them.

After all, they sell books, too.

The Homecoming

He came into his office with such an exuberant air that Miss Nolan, his secretary, knew instantly that the lunch had been a success, that the long negotiations were over, that somehow he had pulled off the deal.

She said breathlessly, just so that he could have the pleasure of telling her, "How did it go, Mr. Stevens?"

"Wonderful, Millie!" Wilbur Stevens sailed his hat at the rack. He missed, but he didn't care. "I guess the third martini did it. Anyway, it's all set. They'll take fifteen thousand motors at twenty bucks apiece. Cavanagh said he'll confirm the order in writing by messenger this afternoon." He gave an excited laugh that was almost boyish. "Gosh, I never dreamed I'd get away with it. They've always bo ght their small electrical stuff from Monarch." He ran his hand through his dark, rumpled hair, his eyes sparkled. "But this time—"

"Oh, Mr. Stevens!" Miss Nolan's rather homely face was bright with enthusiasm. "I'm so happy for you!"

Wilbur Stevens had picked up the family photograph from his desk, was gazing at it fondly. "Thanks, Millie. I knew you'd be pleased." He put the photograph down. "Say, is old B.J. in? I can hardly wait to see his face when he hears about this. No, hold it." He stopped her as she reached for the telephone. "Think I'll wait until the confirmation comes in. Then I'll just walk in and lay it on his desk. Three hundred thousand dollars! Biggest deal I ever—" He checked himself, grinning. "You don't think I'm dreaming, do you?"

"I've never seen you wider awake, Mr. Stevens!"

Wilbur Stevens pulled out his wallet suddenly. "Listen, Millie, I hate to ask you to run personal errands, but this time— Well, down at Beaumont's—you know, the big jewelers there on the avenue—there's a lady's wristwatch. Platinum, set with little diamonds. I have the identification number right here in my wallet. Kept it ever since one day when Mrs. Stevens and I were window-shopping and she admired it. Tell Mr. Blake—he's the manager and he knows me—tell him I want it on approval. Or one just like it. And that I'll come in and pay for it tomorrow—if the lady likes it."

"Oh, Mr. Stevens!" Miss Nolan sounded thrilled. "Of course she'll like it."

"Here." He handed her the number and the fifty-dollar bill that he kept hidden under his identification card, for emergencies. "Stop at a florist's, too, will you? Get me a flower of some kind to go with it—maybe an orchid. Heck, make it two orchids! And get yourself a flower too!"

When she was gone, he sat down at his desk, pulled a scratch pad toward him. He had already figured his commission a dozen times in his head, but he wanted to see the numerals written out, black on white, real, unmistakable.

He stared at the total, fascinated. It was by far the largest single sum he had ever earned. He crumpled the paper slowly, trying to visualize Barbara's face when he handed her the boxes containing wristwatch and orchids. He had thought of telephoning her from the restaurant, but had resisted the impulse. Better to tell her personally.

Not that Barbara cared much about money as such. But there were so many small debts to be cleaned up. The old washing machine to be replaced. Maybe a new refrigerator, one with an ice-cube machine. There was the dream, so long deferred now, of converting the sun deck into an extra bedroom. Or how about a new car? Or what about painting the whole house?

He laughed out loud suddenly, amused and delighted at the torrent of expensive ideas that flashed through his mind. They wouldn't rush things, he decided; everybody's needs would be taken into consideration.

He leaned back, focusing on each of the children in turn. Phyllis, the fourteen-year-old, temperamental, pretty—like her mother. Somewhat self-centered at the moment, but maybe that was part of the miraculous transformation from child into woman. What about a new school for Phyllis, a school—if there was such a thing—that would teach thoughtfulness, gentleness, dignity, along with history and algebra? Why not? A really good school.

The boys needed no such educational refinements—at least, not yet. Johnny and Michael, eleven and nine respectively, devoted friends, passionate enemies, baseball fanatics, television addicts, comic-book devourers, present barbarians, and future custodians of the universe. Michael might like a microscope; he had a mysterious urge to collect bugs and beetles, which he kept, to the despair of his mother, in containers that never contained them for long. Or would it be better to take both the boys fishing in Canada this summer? Just the three of them for one blissful, masculine week.

And then there was Barbie. Wilbur Stevens' face softened at the thought of his seven-year-old. He would have denied it, had anyone asked if he had a preference among his children. But there was something about Barbie. Something about her snub nose, skinned knees, flying braids, and insatiable eagerness to be a part of everything that went on. Something that touched his heart.

Life was not always easy for Barbie. The boys scorned, deplored, and excluded her as a mere girl. Phyllis treated her with the remote condescension of visiting royalty. But she never seemed to resent the snubs or the exclusions.

What to get for Barbie? A bicycle? A puppy? Maybe a summer camp where she could mingle happily with her own contemporaries, safe for a while from the slings and arrows of outrageous siblings? It would take some thought.

Wilbur Stevens looked at his watch. It was after three o'clock. The messenger could hardly arrive before four. He pulled a folder of unanswered correspondence toward him, then pushed it away. He was too excited to work. So why not go down to the barbershop in the lobby of the building, get the haircut he had been needing? No use fidgeting around here.

In an hour he was back. Miss Nolan had the wristwatch and the flowers ready for his inspection.

"They're fine," he told her. "Just right. That gardenia looks awfully nice on you too. Messenger come yet?"

"Not yet, Mr. Stevens."

"Give a shout when he does, will you?"

Miss Nolan permitted herself a daring flight of fancy. "I'll probably turn a cartwheel!"

But the messenger did not come. At four-forty-five, Wilbur Stevens said, a little uneasily, "Check with the reception desk, Millie. Maybe they're holding it out there."

He waited, tapping his fingers on the blotter, feeling a small chill wind of apprehension blow between his shoulder blades. Miss Nolan reappeared, her face reflecting some of the anxiety he felt. "Nothing at the reception desk, Mr. Stevens."

Wilbur Stevens moved the square, green florist's box until it was exactly centered on the blotter. "Better get Cavanagh on the phone, I think."

But again the results were negative. "Mr. Cavanagh is in a conference," Miss Nolan reported. "At least, that's what his secretary says." Her voice trailed off uncertainly.

"Leave word for him to call me back. Tell her I'll wait right here for the call."

He broke off, hearing the panic in his own voice, not wanting Miss Nolan to hear it too. He said slowly, "You'd better give Mrs. Stevens a ring, too, Millie. Tell her I won't be on the usual train. Tell her I don't know how late I'll be."

He didn't want to speak to Barbara himself. Not yet. Not until he knew.

At five-thirty another call to Cavanagh's office received the same answer. At five-fifty they tried once more. This time the message was different. Mr. Cavanagh had left for the day.

Miss Nolan said, over the gardenia pinned so bravely to her shoulder, "Shall I try to get him at home, Mr. Stevens?"

He shook his head. "He wouldn't be there yet. But look up his home number for me, Millie. He lives right here in town. Then you run along."

"I'm in no hurry, Mr. Stevens. I—I have nothing to do."

He knew what she was trying to say. That she was sorry. That she was on his side. That she would sit there until midnight, if it would do any good.

"Thanks, Millie," he said, "but there's no point in both of us staying. I'm sure everything will be all right. You go along."

When she was gone, he moved over to the window. A chill twilight was settling over the city. If the deal were off, surely Cavanagh would have told him. He wouldn't just try to dodge. Or—would he?

Abruptly he turned, picked up the phone, dialed Cavanagh's home number. For a full minute he waited. No answer.

He put the phone down slowly. Cavanagh was a bachelor. He might go home or he might not. Probably stop for a drink somewhere. The Coq d'Or? Mulvaney's?

Wilbur Stevens pushed some papers into his briefcase. He picked up the small package that contained the wristwatch, hesitated, then dropped it into the top desk drawer. It wasn't his; he hadn't earned it—yet. The flowers? Well, he would have to take the flowers. Perhaps the cause for celebration still existed. Of course it did! His mouth tightened. One thing certain, he wasn't going home until he found out.

Cavanagh was not at the Coq d'Or. He wasn't at Mulvaney's, either. At seven o'clock he tried Cavanagh's home number again. Still no answer. He decided to eat something and try again at eight. If he missed the 8:07 train, he knew, he would have to wait for the 9:55, a miserable local that took over an hour to get to his station. But such inconvenience seemed a minor matter now.

He ate in a cafeteria—or rather, tried to eat. His mind kept doubling back like a frightened rabbit, selecting and then rejecting theories, possibilities, explanations. Had Cavanagh exceeded his authority? Surely not. Had some doubt arisen in his mind as to the quality of the motors, or delivery dates? Impossible. Had he simply forgotten to send the confirmation? That was it. After the three martinis Cavanagh drank at lunch, a minor lapse of memory was certainly possible.

At eight o'clock he telephoned again. And again at nine. Still no answer. Then, suddenly, he remembered that Cavanagh had said something about a weekly poker game at The Athletic Club. Maybe a phone call would find him there.

It did. Cavanagh came to the phone, a little thick of speech, a little impatient. Then abruptly embarrassed, and covering the embarrassment with a kind of hollow heartiness.

"Will? That you? F' gosh sakes, never got a chance to call you back, tied up all afternoon! Look, Will, this is a heck of a thing, but— Well, I saw Blodget after lunch, told him about the order I'd given you, and the old boy just hit the ceiling! Seems his son-in-law's been living for years on the commission he gets from Monarch . . . What? Yeah, that's right, Blodget's son-in-law is a salesman for Monarch! So what could I do, Will? I can't afford to antagonize— Well, I just had to sit down and write you a note saying it was no soap, the deal was off. You'll get it in the morning. Boy, I feel rotten about the whole thing. But one of these days we'll make it up to you. No hard feelings, are there, Will? Look, why don't you let me buy you a drink after work tomorrow? Why don't—"

But Wilbur Stevens had hung up.

It was after eleven when his train got in. He walked home from the station, the box of orchids under his arm, his footsteps loud in the quiet streets. Around him, the damp night air. Overhead, the cool indifferent glitter of the stars. And inside him, still, the dull, sick ache that was like a clenched fist just below his breastbone.

Soon he would be home now. It would be a relief to tell Barbara, have someone to share the disappointment with, someone who would understand. Or could she? Could even Barbara understand? He knew she would say all the comforting things. That it was only money. That they hadn't lost anything, really, except something they had never had. That it didn't matter.

She would say those things, and by saying them prove that she didn't really understand. It wasn't just the loss of the money. It was the bitter taste of failure, the soul-shrinking sense that he hadn't been equal to the task. If he had done his job as a salesman, Cavanagh would have fought for the agreement with his own superiors. But he hadn't really done that good a selling job. He had relied too much on the convivial approach. He had put his faith in the third martini. And it had let him down.

He turned the familiar corner. His house sat there behind the picket fence, friendly, ordinary, the dingy paint and the inevitable signs of wear and tear softened by the kindly night. Barbara had left the porch light on for him. She always did.

He stood for a moment with his hand on the gate, feeling the tide of disenchantment surge within him. What was it all about, anyway? What did it all prove? What was he—Wilbur Stevens—doing here on a fragment of spherical rock hurtling through endless caverns of space? He and the other faceless millions. For what purpose did he exist, to what unimaginable end did he live and breathe? Why? Why?

He felt a sudden inarticulate yearning to cry aloud his grief, his sorrow, his loneliness. But who would hear him, who would come to his aid? *I thought I had Cavanagh sold*, he said to himself wearily, *but I didn't.*

At the foot of the porch steps, something gleamed. Michael's bicycle; he had forgotten to put it away again. Wilbur Stevens carried it up the steps, propped it beside the door. He let himself in. The house was dim and quiet. Everyone was asleep.

In the upper hall, at the head of the stairs, a night-light burned. Here the bedroom Phyllis occupied was opposite the boys' room, and thumbtacked to each door, he saw, was a hand-lettered notice. The one on Phyllis' door said, primly but firmly, NO ADMITTANCE! The one on the boys' door said, PRIVATE! KEEP OUT! THIS MEANS YOU!

Wilbur Stevens stared at them somberly. *They know*, he thought. *They know already that you can't trust anyone, you have to rely on yourself. They think it's just a game, another way of teasing Barbie, but it's not a game. It's the way things are.*

Moving on down the hall, he saw that a small rectangle of paper was also pinned to Barbie's door. Well, naturally, if the other demanded privacy, what could she do but demand it too? He leaned closer. It said, in Barbie's wavy script, WEL-COME—ENNYONE.

Wilbur Stevens straightened up slowly, a sudden tightness in his throat. He opened the door and went in. Light from a street lamp cast a dim glow over the narrow bed, the tumbled bedclothes, the small, pajama-clad figure. Face serene, braids dark against the pillow, Barbie slept.

And standing there, looking down at her, Wilbur Stevens knew that he had found his answer—all the answer he needed. Here it was, in his own small child, the spirit that refused to accept rejection, that expected the best from people, and would ultimately get the best—because it offered the best. Here it was, summed up in two words: Welcome—anyone.

He bit his lip, feeling the defeatism drain out of him, knowing that if in all his ordinary, uncertain life he did no more than help transmit this spirit, he had no cause for complaint, no reason to despair.

From under his arm he took the florist's box, opened it, carefully separated one of the fragile flowers, put it on the chair beside the bed. He tiptoed out and closed the door.

In the darkness of their bedroom, Barbara stirred. "Will?"

"Yes." He sat down on the edge of the bed, slipped his hand into hers, felt her carry it to her warm cheek. He put the other orchid beside her pillow. "Here, I brought you a flower."

"Why, Will—it's an orchid!" She sounded amazed and delighted. "But what's it for?"

"It's for you," he said, and kissed her.

She was still holding his hand. He felt her fingers tighten. "What a wonderful ending to a long day! How did it go for you?"

Wilbur Stevens bent down and pulled the laces on his right shoe. "It was all right," he said. "It was fine. It was a very useful day."

X

I've never been able to understand men who feel uneasy if their wives work. Or threatened if their wives make more money than they do. If my wife made more money than I do, I'd be entranced. In fact, I'm entranced when she makes *any* money, which on occasion, I'm happy to say, she does.

Families where wives work now seem to be the rule, not the exception. Some people link this dolefully to erosion of morality or the decline of family life in this country, but I don't think it's a valid connection. Wives who work probably add more to overall family welfare (and to their own self-esteem) by working than by staying home. Nothing wrong with staying home either, if economics permit. It all depends on individual preferences and circumstances.

The one time when the choice becomes difficult is when the children are very small. Babies, I'm sure, get bored like anyone else; they need the stimulus and challenge and reassurance that constant attention from a loving adult can bring. I think it's probably impossible to "spoil" a small baby.

They soak up affection and attention like little sponges.

But the loving adult doesn't necessarily have to be the biological parent. As you'll see in the story that follows.

The Lie

Driving to the station that Saturday afternoon under the gray March sky, Len Harrison felt his sense of depression deepen. Behind him, his son, Jimmy, filled the station wagon with six-year-old exuberance. Beside him, Miss Sims sat quietly, hands folded in her lap, except when she raised one hand now and then to smooth a strand of graying hair into place under her sensible hat. Her face was calm, as controlled as always. *There's no point in feeling grim about it,* Len told himself sharply. *Leaving was her idea, her choice. Why let it bother you?*

But it did bother him all the same.

In the back seat Jimmy had somehow contrived to unfasten the clasps of Miss Sims' suitcase. "Gosh, Missie! Do you have to take all these clothes for just a little *trip?*"

Miss Sims glanced briefly over her shoulder. "Close it up, please, Jimmy. You know better than that."

It was amazing, Len Harrison thought for the thousandth time, *how she could control this tornado of a small boy with a quiet word or a glance.* His parents certainly couldn't seem to do it. *Darn it all,* Len Harrison thought, *why does it have to end like this?* Everything seemed to have come about so quickly. Thursday, as usual, had been Miss Sims' day off. On Friday, innocent-looking enough in its neatly lettered blue envelope, the letter for her arrived from Philadelphia. The next morning, quietly but definitely, she told the Harrisons that she would be leaving them to take another job.

Her explanation was simple and forthright. The people in

Philadelphia, she said, had been urging her for some time to come to them. Now they had made an offer that she didn't feel she could refuse. And so . . .

"I wouldn't have believed it," Margot Harrison said fiercely to her husband. "I never thought she cared that much about *money*. I thought she loved the children, both of them—especially Jimmy!"

Len Harrison had rubbed his forehead ruefully. "She *is* fond of the children; I don't think there's any doubt about that. But she's a single woman, honey, and not getting any younger. If these people can pay her so much more, you certainly can't blame her for thinking about herself. After all—"

"Oh, Len!" his wife cried despairingly. "You're always making excuses for other people. What about her sense of loyalty? Don't you think she owes us something? How can she just—just walk out like this?"

"She isn't walking out, exactly. She's offered to stay until we find somebody else."

"I don't want her to stay," Margot said grimly. "Not now. It would be tense and—and miserable. If she's going, she'd better go. Today. This very day. You can put her on the afternoon train to the city."

"What'll we do next week? What about your job?"

"I'll just have to work at home until we can get somebody else."

"What are we going to tell the kids?"

Margot hesitated. "Barbara won't mind so much. She's too young to understand. But Jimmy . . ." She bit her lip. "Well, we'd better just say that Missie has to go away on a trip and let him think she'll be back."

Jimmy, who gave his heart so readily and so completely. Jimmy, who had given it to Miss Sims—or Missie, as he called her—the very first day she arrived.

It was the day of Margot's return from the hospital with a brand-new baby girl. Len had asked the employment agency in the city to send someone to help with Jimmy and the household chores until Margot was herself again. "Someone reliable," he had said. "Someone who can just take over for a couple of weeks." They sent Miss Sims.

She was not at first sight a very impressive-looking person. She was small and rather plain except for her eyes, which were a clear, candid gray. Her accent sounded faintly British; later they learned she was born in Canada. Her age might have been anywhere between thirty-five and forty-five; it was hard to tell.

Her references were excellent, although it was evident from them that she never stayed long in one position. She didn't talk much about herself. She didn't show much emotion either; there was something very reserved, very disciplined, about her. But there was warmth beneath the discipline. Both Harrisons sensed it, and their son, made uneasy by the arrival of the new baby, was drawn to it instantly.

"Oh, Len," Margot whispered that first night, "she's marvelous. If only we could keep her!"

"What would you do?" he had asked, teasing her. "Go back to your old job?"

"Believe me," said Margot fervently, "if I knew the children were safe and happy, I would. We could use the extra money to pay Miss Sims."

That was the way things worked out. Miss Sims did agree to stay; Margot did go back to work. Before her marriage she had been a dress designer, a good one. The months slipped by; the family seemed to be running like a well-oiled machine—until the day the letter came from Philadelphia.

Now the station was in sight, a handful of Saturday passengers waiting on the long platform. Len Harrison eased the car into his usual parking place under a great willow tree whose branches made black tracery against the sky. He reached out slowly and cut the ignition. *Queer,* he was thinking, *queer and a little sad how easily relationships were broken or reached an end.* All the shared laughter, all the common interests, all the woven threads of living—they should add up to some kind of permanency. Evidently they didn't.

Abruptly there came into his head a scene from the early part of the week. Was it Tuesday? No, Wednesday. It had been the children's bedtime, and Miss Sims, who was stronger than she looked, picked them both up for the climb up the stairs. Margot held out her arms first to Barbie and then to

Jimmy, but both of them, giggling and laughing, clung to Miss Sims. And Margot said, also laughing, "Well, chicks, it's easy to see who comes first with you around here!" But Miss Sims put the children down quickly. "Go to your mother, Jimmy," she said. "You, too, Barbara." And, as usual they obeyed her.

The car door clicked open and Miss Sims stepped out. "Thank you, Mr. Harrison. Thank you for everything."

"When'll you be back, Missie?" Jimmy cried, bouncing on the seat. "When'll you be *back?*"

Miss Sims gave him her quiet smile. "I'll sit down tomorrow, Jimmy, and write you a letter. You'll find it when you come home from school on Monday. That's a promise."

Len Harrison said, "Why don't you wait here in the car until the train comes?"

But Miss Sims had already opened the rear door. "No," she said. "No, thank you. I'd really rather you didn't wait."

She turned quickly and walked away from them, shoulders set against the weight of the suitcase. She crossed the damp black cinders, a resolute and oddly lonely little figure. She came to the platform steps and mounted them. She did not look back.

"Daddy," said Jimmy, "this fell out of Missie's suitcase when I opened it. Do you think she wants it?"

Len Harrison stared down at the blue envelope, at the neatly printed address, at the Philadelphia postmark. And all at once he knew. Unmistakably he knew.

He drew out the folded sheet of notepaper and saw that it was blank. There was no letter from Philadelphia. There never had been such a letter. Miss Sims had sent herself an envelope, that was all—to justify leaving. Because she felt it would be better for Jimmy and Barbara. Because she felt they were beginning to love her too much.

Len Harrison felt his throat tighten. How often had she done this, removed herself because she feared she was beginning to receive affection that by her strict standards should belong only to parents? How often had she exiled herself—not because she wanted to or had to, but because she thought it was the right thing to do?

He looked down the long platform at the small figure walking away from them into emptiness, into loneliness. He reached for his pen; on the piece of paper he scrawled two hasty lines. "Jimmy," he said, "take this to Missie, will you?"

"Okay!" In a flash the child was out of the car. Across the cinders he raced. "Missie! Missie! Wait!" Up onto the platform. His father saw him offer the note. Sixteen words: "Missie, there's no such thing as too much love. Come on back here where you belong."

Standing on the platform under the leaden sky, Miss Sims read the message. For a moment she did not move. Then carefully she folded it, put it into her pocket. She picked up her suitcase and offered her free hand to Jimmy. Together they started back down the platform.

In the car Len Harrison found himself gripping the steering wheel hard. He made his hands relax. He opened the car door and stepped out. As he stood there waiting, he noticed that the branches above his head were not so bleak and bare after all. They were blurred with green. They were hazy with the promise of spring.

XI

"Two things," wrote the philosopher Immanuel Kant, "fill the mind with ever-increasing awe and wonder: the starry heavens above me and the moral law within me."

As a child I was not too concerned with the moral law, but the starry heavens, arching over land and sea, made a deep impression on me. My father was interested in astronomy, and we used to lie on the beach on moonless nights and watch the constellations, solemn and splendid, wheel around the North Star. I loved the names of the stars—Arcturus, Aldebaran, Vega—and would have stayed out all night watching them if I could. Especially in August when the Perseids came, meteorite showers that filled the night with shooting stars, each drawing its golden streak across the heavens.

The concept that struck my young mind with the greatest impact was not so much infinite distance, which I couldn't grasp, as the idea of almost unimaginable size, which I could. Once, when we were talking about the giant star Betelgeuse that perches on the shoulder of Orion, Father told me that if there were a man on Betelgeuse whose size was proportionate to a man on earth, he could swallow our sun without even burning his throat. This made me feel uncomfortably small, and I told Father that it did. "Never mind," he said, "you can think about Betelgeuse, but it can't think about you."

I remember how Scorpio glittered in the summer sky, the sweep of its mighty tail reaching almost to the horizon, the great red star Antares glowing like a fiery heart. I used to imagine sometimes that the sky was a bottomless indigo ocean and all the stars were fish (Antares was a redfish), and that if I just had a line long enough I might be able to catch one or two. Years later, when radio telescopes began to be developed, scientists really could fish in the endless seas of space. They never seemed to get a bite, but one day, thinking about it, I said to myself, "What if . . . ?"

The old storyteller's reaction: *what if . . . ?*

The Signal

"It was a signal," Brad Manton said. He pounded his fist softly on the kitchen table. "I don't care what they say. It was a signal!"

He leaned back and ran one hand through his short blond hair. He was only twenty-six, but at the moment he looked older. The light slanted down, accenting the lines of tension and fatigue in his face.

His wife came and stood behind his chair and put her arms around him for a moment. She was a slender girl, dark haired with gentle eyes. She said, reproachfully, "You haven't eaten a thing."

He reached up for her hand. "Not hungry, I guess. I just feel so frustrated, so . . ."

"You're too intense about things, Brad. Especially this job of yours."

"Look," he said, "it's the most exciting job there is. For a limited time every day, I'm given the biggest radio telescope in the world to play with. What's my territory? The whole uncharted universe! Just to listen, to listen for something out there in that . . . that endlessness. Something that might indicate that somewhere, at some time, there were beings intelligent enough to have sent radio signals pulsing through space. How can I help being excited? It's more than just science. There's a kind of yearning in it. It's like fishing in the ocean of time with a line ten billion miles long. It's like wishing on a star, and then waiting for the star to answer!"

Her hands were quiet on his shoulders. "And today you really think you got an answer?"

"I got a pattern. A repetitive pattern. Like this." He rapped twice on the table, then three times, then once. "It was impulse, impulse, pause; impulse, impulse, impulse, pause; impulse. Then the pattern repeated itself. Very faint. Very far away. But *repeated!*"

"And then?"

"Nothing. Just the usual static. But it wasn't something I dreamed or imagined. It was there, all right. It's on the tape."

His wife moved over to the window and stared out into the summer night. "Could you tell how far this—this signal came?"

He shook his head. "There are countless stars in any given area of the sky. Five hundred light-years away. A thousand. Ten thousand. Some must have planets like ours."

"Then the message—if it was a message—might have been sent ten thousand years ago?"

"Yes. But that's only a tick of the cosmic clock."

"What did the others think?"

"Oh, Barclay said that a single repetition of a cycle didn't prove anything. Cunningham was more sarcastic. He said that if it was a signal, it must have come from the inhabitants of a pretty backward planet because evidently they were trying to tell us that two plus three equals one. And I'm afraid he had a point. Mathematical laws must be the same throughout the universe. An ascending or a descending sequence might make some sense. But I don't understand two and then three and then one."

"Brad," said his wife, "take me out in the garden for a minute."

They went out into the blue-velvet night and stood close together, shoulders touching, looking up at the great vault where the stars flowed like powdered diamonds. "Brad, if you were trying to send a message across billions of miles and thousands of years, I don't think you'd settle for some little mathematical truism. You'd try for something bigger, much bigger. And I don't think you'd aim at another mind. You'd aim at another heart."

He stared at her face, luminous in the starlight. "What do you mean?"

"That sequence you heard," she said. "Two, three, one. Shall I tell you what it meant to me? Right away? The moment I heard it?"

"Yes," he said. "Tell me."

"It's in the Bible," she said. "That same sequence. A simple statement but a tremendous one: *Where two or three are gathered together . . . there am I in the midst of them* (Matthew 18:20). Don't you see? If it's true at all, it must be true everywhere. Two or three persons, two or three anything—it wouldn't matter, would it? God would be there just as he is here with us right now in this garden."

A strange tingling seemed to move along Brad Manton's spine. Above him the great constellations blazed down through unimaginable distances, through endless eons of time. He reached for his wife's hand. "Yes," he said huskily, "you're right. That's the way it always has been. That's the way it still is."

XII

Sometimes the elements that make up a story seem to come from all directions, like winding paths that meet in a wood. Sometimes the elements are events, sometimes they're people. They may have absolutely nothing to do with one another, really, but some curious chemistry in the storyteller's mind takes and blends and fuses them until a new entity emerges. An entity called a story.

I once had a friend named James Ramsey Ullman. A good writer. And a fine mountain climber. His most successful book was a novel called *The White Tower*, about some man-killing peak in the Alps and the people who attempted to conquer it. Jim was an interesting fellow. He had a pet monkey, I remember, that used to scamper about his New York apartment and perch on the mantelpiece. And he had a little house in Bermuda where we'd visit him sometimes. There was a cistern in the cellar to catch rainwater because Bermuda has so little water. In the cistern were little fish whose job it was to eat up mosquito larvae and keep the water clean enough to drink. I found this quite fascinating.

Well, anyway, Jim used to talk a lot about mountains and glaciers and things. Path number one.

Then when I was in college in England I had a friend named George McGhee, who later became an oil tycoon and was named ambassador to various countries and served as undersecretary of state. While we were at Oxford, George built what may well have been the first seismograph ever constructed in Britain. The French government asked George, who was only about twenty-two, to bring his gadget down to North Africa and look for oil in the Sahara. So he did. I don't think he found any oil, but he stayed in the desert for a while, out of touch with everything. Path number two.

Then later I had a friend whose wife was unfaithful to him. When he found out about it, he was terribly unhappy and upset. She asked him to forgive her, and something in him wanted very much to do just that, but he couldn't quite do it. So both of them were miserable. Path number three.

The three paths wandered around in my head for a good many years. Finally they came together.

The Discovery

I am always glad to get back to Paris, and I was particularly glad this last time. I had been in the Sahara for six weeks with a crew of French geologists, doing a series of articles on oil hunters. It had been six weeks of blazing sun and burning sand, tinned water, no news, and excitable Arabs. But now I was in Paris again. I had no particular plans beyond a long, hot bath, and a good dinner. After that—well, something would turn up. It did.

When I went into the hotel lounge at seven-thirty, the first person I saw was Tony Ashurst. We had gone to the same school, Tony Ashurst and I, and to the same college. I had always liked him, even though some people said having too much money had spoiled him. I didn't agree. He had the nerve not to work—it takes quite a lot in our society—and he had plenty of physical courage.

Mountaineering was his passion. He had climbed most of the great peaks, including one in Peru that had never been scaled before. But he never talked much about his accomplishments. He was quite shy, really, and sensitive and proud. He looked rather like a Spaniard with his dark hair and sunburned skin and intense eyes, but he was pure Philadelphia.

He was light and wiry, the way most great climbers are. Usually there was a kind of tension about him, but now, sitting alone at the bar sipping a glass of lime-flavored Perrier water, he looked almost boyishly happy. "Why, Jim," he said, when I walked up to him, "it's good to see you!"

"You too," I said, and hesitated, wondering whether or not to ask about Karen, his wife. I had heard a rumor that their marriage was not going smoothly. I decided not to risk it. "What've you been doing?"

He looked surprised. "You mean you haven't seen the papers?"

"Where I've been," I said, "there weren't any papers." I told him about the oil series.

"Then you haven't heard of the Ashurst discovery?"

I shook my head. "It wasn't oil, by any chance?"

He smiled and said, "No, it . . . Look, I'd like to talk to you, Jim, if you have the time. Will you have a drink?"

"Same as yours," I said. "Let's find a place to sit."

We went over to a table. Tony looked at me for a moment and then he said, "You know, Jim, you're the first person I've met who didn't begin by *asking* me about this business. Since you know nothing about it, I'd like to try an experiment with you. I'd like to tell the story from the beginning—something I haven't been able to do with anyone else—and see what you make of it."

My drink arrived. I had all the time in the world. "Go ahead," I said.

After a moment he said, "I feel a little hesitant about this. You'll see why. But even so, I feel like sharing this story with someone, someone I've known for a long time. And you're the first person I've found that I *could* tell it to. Aren't you flattered?"

"Very," I said. As a matter of fact, I was.

He squared his shoulders a little, like a diver on a high board. "It really began four years ago," he said, "when Karen and I were married."

I remembered their wedding; it was the social event of the season, and for a year or two the marriage went very well. Tony and Karen traveled constantly; they circled the earth on one long honeymoon.

But then things began to change. It wasn't that they had grown bored with each other physically or anything like that. It was just that every man needs a sense of achievement—even if it comes only from conquering jagged masses of rock—and Karen hated the mountains.

She was afraid of heights. Climbing terrified her. Tony tried to make her see that being afraid was no disgrace, that fear could be overcome. Karen wanted no part of mountain climbing.

She never tried to stop Tony from going—he was careful to give her credit for that. At first he went off on short trips, weekend climbs, but it was no good. Karen wouldn't say a word, but he knew she was upset, and this ruined everything. He felt guilty about leaving her, guilty about pursuing the only real interest he had outside their marriage.

He looked at me with a puzzled expression. "Can you see how that might be?" he asked.

"Nobody likes the person who makes him feel guilty," I said, "or weak."

He nodded. "Last winter, as you know," he said, "I organized that expedition to the Andes. Winter here, of course, is summer down there. I told Karen that I didn't want her with me. I told her she could wait in Philadelphia or London or Paris, but I didn't want her anywhere in South America. I was going to try to be the first man to climb La Dolorosa, and I didn't want any distractions. Karen didn't say much, but I knew she was hurt and angry. I almost called the expedition off. But in the end I told myself that that would just be—as you said—a sign of weakness."

"As it turned out," he said finally, "I was away even longer than the three months I had planned. After we climbed La Dolorosa the weather held, and we took a shot at El Capitan. We didn't make it, but," he grinned, "we came darned close. Next time, maybe ..." He paused and sipped his drink. "While I was gone, Karen stayed here, in Paris. I came back in June, feeling pretty good about everything. A little penitent, maybe, for having kept her waiting so long, but the trouble was—," he hesitated, not looking at me, and I saw his fingers tighten around the stem of his glass—, "she had found someone else."

I said nothing. I could think of nothing to say.

"She told me herself, the night I got back. She was miserable about it, really. She told me because she was sure that if she didn't, someone we knew would. She said she supposed she had done it to punish me for leaving her. She was awfully sorry, she said; she wasn't even infatuated with this other fellow any more. She—she asked me to forgive her."

It was cool there in the bar, but there were tiny beads of sweat on Tony Ashurst's forehead.

"Heaven knows," he said, "I wanted to—I tried. I told myself I had had this coming. She had been no more faithless to me, in a way, than I had been to her. Karen's a beautiful girl, high-spirited, proud. I could understand it all, rationally. But emotionally—," he shook his head—, "I couldn't take it. We weren't man and wife any more; we were like strangers. That went on for months. Then, about three weeks ago, I told her we were through. I said I thought we should get a divorce."

Somewhere across the room a woman was laughing; there was a subdued murmur of conversation.

"The next day," Tony went on, "Karen asked me to take her away—to the mountains. She said we ought to give our marriage one more chance. She thought, I guess, that if she made this—this surrender to my interests, perhaps I could make a concession as well. Anyway, we went. I didn't plan to do any real climbing, of course, but I thought if we got up fairly high, around ten or eleven thousand feet, well away from the tourist resorts, we might gain a better perspective of our problem. I thought we'd spend a few days tramping around on the Lac de Glace, the glacier above Stehl."

He paused again. He wasn't filling in the details, but I could see it all, see them setting out with their expensive luggage in their handsome car, giving an impression of wealth and happiness, but actually miserable.

Tony rubbed his chin, his eyes not seeing the room or people around us. "Glaciers," he said, "they're really fascinating. They still cover ten percent of the globe, you know, and there's evidence that they once covered thirty. Down in the south polar regions they say the ice cap is two miles thick."

I nodded impatiently. I was not interested in glaciers. I wanted to hear what had happened to this man and his wife.

"The Lac de Glace," he said, "is the Piedmont type, a large, nearly motionless ice sheet. There's almost no drainage; evaporation balances snowfall. There are some crevasses, of course, but nothing really dangerous. It seemed a good place to go ..."

They stayed at the only inn Stehl had to offer, a funny old place called the Lion d'Or. Every day they took their lunch and climbed up to the glacier. The weather was superb; the air crystal clear, the sun almost hot. They were polite and considerate to each other. But they were companions, not lovers.

On the fourth day they picked a place to eat their lunch where a ridge of ice sheltered them from the wind. The view was magnificent. In the distance they could see both Mont Blanc and Monte Rosa. In front of them the glacier sloped down to a deep crevasse ten or twelve yards across. Tony handed his binoculars to his wife. "Take a look," he said.

She raised the glasses to her eyes, but she didn't try to focus them, and suddenly he knew that she wasn't looking at anything.

"Tony," she said, "it's not going to work, is it?"

He felt miserable. He wanted to tell her that everything was going to be all right, that the past was over and done with. But he couldn't, and suddenly Karen dropped the glasses and covered her face with her hands. He reached for the glasses, but it was too late. The binoculars slid down the ice and disappeared into the crevasse.

Karen looked up, stricken. "Oh, Tony, how awful!" she said. "I'm terribly sorry."

"That's all right," he told her. "They can be replaced."

"But they were your father's."

Tony's father had made a ceremony of giving the glasses to him the day he was to climb the Matterhorn for the first time.

He got up, moved carefully to the edge of the crevasse, and looked down. He couldn't see the bottom, but he saw the binoculars lying on a shelf some seventy or eighty feet down. He could hardly believe his luck; he had been sure they were gone for good. He called to Karen that he was going down after them.

"No!" she said, getting up, and all her fear of the mountains was in her voice.

"There's nothing to it," he said. "I'll use the rope—anchor it with the ax."

She came and stood beside him and looked down quickly into the greenish depth. Her face was very pale. "All right," she said. "But if you go, take me with you."

He stared at her. "You want to go down *there?*"

She said, "I want to be with you."

They stood there for perhaps ten seconds, facing each other.

"All right," Tony said. "It won't be dangerous if you do what I tell you. And I'll tell you this, too—when we come back up, you won't be afraid any more."

"I don't care about that," she said. "All I care about is being with you."

Tony let her down first, slowly, carefully. Karen was rigid with fear, but something kept her from crying out—something stronger than fear.

Fifteen minutes later they were standing together on the shelf where the binoculars had landed. The sunlight, filtering through the translucent ice, had a weird, undersea quality. Tony picked up the binoculars. "Hullo," he said, "what's that?"

Something that looked like a wire was projecting from the ice wall about twenty feet farther ahead.

He moved along the ledge, holding Karen's hand, until he came close to it. It wasn't wire. It seemed to be frozen rawhide, and it was attached to something in the ice. He could see it plainly behind the surface; it was a thin yellowish rectangle about the size of a playing card.

Our glasses were empty but Tony did not notice. He was too deep in his story.

"I chipped it out and looked at it, while Karen held on to my arm. At first I thought it was bone; then I decided it was some sort of ivory. And it was engraved on both sides—crudely and beautifully and painstakingly engraved—with hunting scenes. There were men with spears and there were the animals they were hunting.

"I stood there, seventy feet below the surface of the Lac de Glace, and I swear to you, Jim, I felt the hair rise on the back of my neck. Because I had seen those animals before, seen them in the cave drawings of southern France. Humpbacked bison, and wooly mammoths with curling tusks, and wooly rhinoceroses—some of them extinct for thousands of years, but painted from life by Neolithic man a hundred centuries ago.

"Then I felt Karen's hand tighten on mine. I glanced up, and I saw what she was looking at. They were not six feet above our heads, Jim. It was as if they were encased in transparent crystal, every detail unaltered, undecayed. The woman—she was a girl, really—was lower down, closer to us. Her face was turned away; I couldn't see it. But I could see her dark hair and the skins she was dressed in and the queer crude leggings she wore. I could even see the little pouch that she had tied to one wrist, almost like a modern handbag.

"Her arms were stretched up toward the man. He was reaching down to her; I could see his face plainly, see the look of love and anguish on it. He was lying on his stomach, one arm reaching down toward the girl. He had something in his hand that looked like a short stick; it may turn out to be a stone ax, handle forward. We don't know yet.

"You don't have to be a mountaineer to reconstruct what happened. Perhaps a snow bridge broke; perhaps she dropped her amulet and was trying to recover it. Anyway, she got herself into a place from which she couldn't get back, and he was trying to rescue her, although he must have known that even a whisper might shake loose the tons of snow poised about them. He went down after her and he had almost reached her when the avalanche came and they died together."

Tony Ashurst stopped speaking, and although the hum of conversation went on around us undiminished, I felt as if we were completely alone.

"I knew," he said after a moment, "that we had made a sensational discovery. I knew that the earliest traces of Troy or Babylon were nothing compared to the antiquity of these two people who had lived in the dawn of time as we know it. But somehow that knowledge didn't impress me much. I didn't think of those two as Neolithic cave dwellers miraculously preserved for thousands of years. I thought of them simply as a man and a woman who had loved each other, who had lived and died for each other. They had been dead for scores of centuries, but their love was still alive. I felt humble and ashamed. I turned to Karen and—" He broke off suddenly.

"Yes?" I asked, prompting him.

He was looking past me, and he was smiling. Karen Ashurst was coming toward us. She was wearing a simple black dress with only one ornament, a yellowish rectangle of ivory suspended around her neck from a thin gold chain. She looked more beautiful than I remembered her.

"Why, Jim," she said to me, "what a nice surprise!"

I stood up slowly. I knew, now, what Tony had been trying to tell me, what the Ashurst discovery really was.

She put her hand on her husband's shoulder. "Sorry I'm late, darling. I'm not interrupting something, am I?"

"A story," I said to her. "But you're not interrupting it. You're the happy ending."

I was glad for them; I was very glad.

XIII

The headquarters of the United Nations in New York City is an impressive place. The flags of more than a hundred nations snapping in the wind that blows off the East River. The handsome gardens with statuary from all over the world. The great gold pendulum just inside the main entrance that swings majestically to and fro, its motion caused—they say—by the rotation of the earth itself.

And then there's a small room called the Meditation Room, where very few people go. I suppose it's the closest the UN, with its multiplicity of religions, could come to a chapel. It's very quiet in there. Once or twice I've sat on one of the backless benches and listened to the silence and wondered how much influence the room might have—if any—on the thoughts or actions of the diplomats who come and go in the busy corridors.

The world never seems to be able to draw back from the brink of self-annihilation. It never quite seems to go over the edge, either. The story that follows, now, was written some time ago and it may be a little dated now.

But not much.

That's the pity of it.

Not much.

One Hour to War

On the third day of the crisis, the old man came to New York. Unannounced, uninvited, he flew in with Mathieson, his quiet selfless secretary. The old man's face was seamed with age and wisdom; he moved stiffly as he descended from the plane. But there was great dignity and purpose in him still.

Waiting for his car, hat pulled down over his eyes, he watched the long lines at the ticket counters. So far there had been no mass exodus, no panic. But already some people were moving out. And it was not surprising, the old man thought. Not when you considered the black headlines, the grim bulletins on radio and television, the conviction growing, hour by hour, that this time the fuse was really lit and hissing, this time the explosion was inevitable. And when it came, New York . . .

He felt a touch on his arm, heard Mathieson's anxious voice. "Car was held up by the traffic, sir. But it's here now." Poor Matty—so devoted, so efficient and such a worrier. With the world about to collapse, he could still be upset because a car was five minutes late.

In the limousine, the old man leaned back wearily. He touched a button at his elbow, and at once the doomlike voice of some newscaster filled the car: ". . . spokesman held out no hope that an open clash could be averted. In this morning's meeting of the Security Council the Soviet delegate made it crystal clear that Russia would consider any military move by

Britain or France an act of war against itself. The British and French made equally clear their determination to support at all costs. . . ."

The old story. Threat and counterthreat. Then the ultimatum, carefully calculated to call a bluff—if it was a bluff. And then, swift and deadly, the chain reaction leading to . . . The old man felt his mind shy away from the thought. Twice he had seen the process lead to global war. This time it would be—annihilation.

The radio voice droned inexorably on: ". . . announced that the armed forces were in a state of complete combat readiness. In New York, a formal announcement of the decision to resort to force is expected within the hour. It will be contained in an address scheduled to be delivered before the General Assembly by the foreign minister of. . . ."

The old man snapped the radio off. It could tell him nothing that he did not already know. Outside, the gray twilight fled past. They crossed the soaring bridge that led to Manhattan, and Mathieson said, worriedly, "Wouldn't you rather go to the hotel first, sir? Rest up a bit before . . ."

The old man shook his head. "There isn't time, Matty."

When they reached the UN buildings, a fine, chill rain had begun to fall. The crowd outside the visitors' entrance was smaller than the old man had anticipated.

He moved, unrecognized, through the heavy glass-and-nickel doors, across the lobby, past the great golden pendulum that marked with its majestic rhythm the slow rotation of the earth. In front of a closed door on the western side of the building he stopped. From his pocket he drew the five identical notes he had written with his own hand on the plane. He handed them to the secretary. "Ask them if they'll meet me in here, Matty."

"*Here,* sir?"

The old man smiled a little. "You might say, it's neutral ground. Also, we're not likely to be disturbed. Tell them . . . tell them it won't take long."

He watched the secretary hurry away. Then he pushed open the door, slowly, and went in.

As he had expected, the Meditation Room was empty. It

was not large: twelve paces long, perhaps, one end narrower than the other so that the blank walls seemed to converge. The indirect lighting was very dim; the silence was profound. Directly ahead of the old man were two backless benches. Beyond them, centered in the thick carpeting, was a block of stone, narrowly rectangular, perhaps four feet high. It was without ornament or inscription of any kind, but from a concealed spotlight overhead a shaft of light fell like a sword blade and glittered on the particles of mica in the polished surface.

He moved forward and sat down stiffly on one of the benches. They would come; he was fairly sure of that. But when they did come . . . he felt the sudden doubt bite into him. What he planned to do seemed so weak, suddenly, so inadequate in the face of the avalanche poised above them all.

He waited and they came. Out of curiosity, perhaps. Certainly out of self-interest. But also out of respect for the old man and the greatness that had filled his life.

One by one they came, alone as requested, and the old man greeted each one quietly. When all were assembled, he moved around the block of stone so that he stood at the far end, facing them."Gentlemen," he said, "thank you for coming."

He could only see their faces dimly. They had divided themselves so that the Briton, the Frenchman, and the American were on one side of him. The Russian and his satellite were on the other. The stone was a granite barrier between them.

"Gentlemen," the old man said, "w⁻ all know, the whole world knows, that time is running out. It is no longer a question of which of you is right. There is right on both sides; that is why it is so hard to reach a solution, or to compromise. But—"

"We have!" The shadowy figure on the old man's left interrupted him furiously. "We have compromised! We have made concessions! The conscience of the free world—"

From the other side of the stone came a fierce whisper: "My country will not submit to threats! We will not yield to force! Never!"

The tall Briton said, in his weary, cultured voice, "I assure you, sir, we have tried everything. Everything . . ."

The old man said slowly, "Have you tried loving one another?"

The question hung in the quiet air. Simple. Enormous.

"It is hard, I know," the old man went on. "And realization comes late, for governments as well as individuals. But this is the true purpose of the United Nations: to turn this ideal into a reality." He moved slightly so that he was facing the Russian. "Even you, sir, have for your objective the betterment of people, is it not so? And not just your people, but all people. If, then, our aims are so similar, how can we take or permit any action that will destroy them?"

Silence sang in the room. There was no answer.

"I wish," said the old man, "that each of you would do me the courtesy of resting his hand for a moment on this stone." He stretched out his own hand, and slowly the others did likewise.

"Originally," the old voice went on, "an altar was a place of sacrifice. Is there any reason why it should not serve today for the sacrifice of self-justification, of arrogance, of pride? We are all guilty of these things, and in our hearts we know it. Perhaps that is why we set this symbol here, although we have never truly consecrated it. This is more than just a stone, gentlemen. It is the future of mankind. Which of you, then, will be the first to draw your hand away?"

Silence again. No one moved. Under the steady shaft of light the Frenchman's thin fingers trembled slightly. The Russian's big fist moved back half an inch, then grew still. The seconds ticked away.

Finally the old man lifted his hand. "I know you have much to do, gentlemen. Thank you, again, for coming here."

When they were gone, he stood motionless for a time. Then he moved over to the bench and sat down. Time passed, but he did not move. An hour went by, and part of another. Once he thought he heard a muffled sound that might have been cheering. But he could not be sure.

He wasn't sure of anything until the door opened and

Mathieson came in. The secretary was breathing hard, almost as if he had been running. He leaned back against the wall, and when he spoke, his voice shook a little. "The speech is over, sir. The foreign minister didn't even—even mention the crisis. He talked about—about the future of his country, and of the world . . ."

The old man nodded without speaking. At last he said, "How's the weather outside, Matty? Is it still raining?"

The secretary shook his head. "It's stopped, now, sir. The stars are out . . ."

The old man stood up slowly. "That's good." He bent down, picked up his hat. He looked once around the quiet room. Sighing, he turned to the door. "I think I am a little tired, Matty. Maybe we ought to be getting along."

XIV

Somebody told me the other night that the short story is coming back. Didn't say back from where. From a kind of partial eclipse, I guess. This person went on to say that little storytelling groups are springing up here and there, where people *listen* to storytellers the way they did for thousands of years. Wouldn't surprise me if this is true. You can play all sorts of electronic games and enjoy them for a while. But there's something cold about them. I don't think they fill the hunger for emotion that all of us feel, the need for contact with flesh and blood, the sense of being led deeper into living.

Anyway, I hope my friend is right.

For a good many years I used to write short fiction for *This Week* magazine, a newspaper supplement that was a part of the Sunday edition in many cities. The fiction editor was Stewart Beach, a wonderful, warm person and a real short-story enthusiast. Stewart loved a story that had atmosphere;

he was always telling me to "turn on the gaslight." Seems to me now that I wrote dozens of stories for him.

They were fun to do because they had to be short—short-shorts, really—which meant that there was no room for mistakes. You had to hit it sharp and quick, like a half-volley in tennis. Good training for a writer. You couldn't waste words.

Here's one that Stewart liked. It does have gaslight in it.

From an Admirer

Sitting quietly in his little herb shop on a crooked street in the shadow of Notre Dame, Doctor Maximus did not look like a very remarkable man. But he was. Five hundred years before, he might have busied himself changing the baser metals into gold. But in the Paris of the nineties, it is said, he worked at a more subtle alchemy. He changed dreams into realities—provided, of course, you could pay.

The man who came into the gaslit shop this early October evening in 1891 was prepared to pay. He stood just inside the door, blotting his forehead with a silk handkerchief although actually the weather was rather cool. He was holding a heart-shaped package tightly under one arm. "You are Monsieur le Docteur Maximus?"

The doctor bowed respectfully.

"I have a problem," said the visitor nervously. "I am told you might help me with it."

"Indeed?" said the doctor mildly. "Who told you that?"

The newcomer glanced around uneasily at the dim shelves, the leathery tortoise dangling from a string, the small stuffed crocodile with its dust-filmed eyes. "Last night we had a dinner guest. A foreign diplomat. First secretary of the—"

"Ah, yes, Pechkoff. It is true I did him a small service."

"He was not very specific, you understand. But after a few glasses of cognac he talked rather freely. I got the impression . . ."

"Yes?"

"That if it weren't for your—er—assistance he would still be married, most unhappily, to his first wife."

Doctor Maximus took off his glasses and polished the spotless lenses. "She died, I believe, poor woman. Quite suddenly."

"Yes," said the visitor, "she did. So suddenly that there was an autopsy. But they discovered nothing wrong."

"Of course not," said Doctor Maximus, smiling gently.

"My wife," said the visitor with a certain agitation, "is a very beautiful woman. Naturally, she has many admirers. She has always ignored them until recently, but now there is one—I don't know which one—a younger man, no doubt. She admits it! She demands that I make some settlement. I will not—"

Doctor Maximus raised his hand. "The details," he murmured, "do not concern me."

The visitor's face was tight and dangerous. "I am not a man to be made a fool of!"

"No," said the doctor, "I can see that."

"Madame," said the visitor abruptly, "is very fond of candy." He unwrapped the heart-shaped package and placed it on the counter. It was a box of chocolates. "I thought perhaps you might—ah—improve the candies at your convenience and then post them to her. She would be very pleased. I have even prepared a card to enclose." He took out a small rectangle of cardboard. On it was printed in neat capitals: FROM AN ADMIRER.

Doctor Maximus took the card and sighed. "My fees are not inconsiderable."

"I did not expect them to be," the visitor said stiffly. He did not flinch when the price was named. He paid it, in gold coins. He blotted his forehead once more with the silk handkerchief. "Will you be able to send the candy tonight?"

"Perhaps," said the doctor noncommittally. "We shall see. And where should it be sent?"

"Ah, yes," said the visitor. "Of course." And he gave Madame's name and address.

Doctor Maximus wrote the information on a slip of paper. Then he scribbled three digits on another slip and handed it over. "You, sir, are customer 322. If there are any difficulties, kindly refer to that number. Not," he added, "that there will be any."

With one hand on the doorknob, the visitor hesitated. "It won't be—," he wet his lips—, "it won't be painful, will it?"

"Not at all," said Dr. Maximus. He peered over his spectacles in a benign and sympathetic fashion. "You seem rather upset. Do you want me to give you something to make you sleep?"

"No, thank you," said the visitor nervously. "I have my own prescription for insomnia: a hot grog before going to bed."

"Ah, yes," said Dr. Maximus. "An excellent habit."

"Good night," said the visitor, opening the door into the narrow, ill-lit street.

"Goodbye," murmured Dr. Maximus.

Taking the box of chocolates in one hand and the slip of paper in the other, he went into the little room at the rear of the shop. From the shelf above his test tubes and retorts he took a big black book, opened it, and looked at the record of the previous transaction. There it was, entered only that afternoon in his spidery handwriting: *Customer 321. Complaint: the usual. Remedy: six drops of the elixir, to be administered in husband's hot grog at bedtime.*

Dr. Maximus sighed. Then, being a man who honored his commitments, he opened the box of chocolates and went to work. There was no great rush. He would post the parcel in the morning.

In the herb shop, as in life, you got just about what you paid for. But his motto was, First Come, First Served.

XV

I wonder, sometimes, how many children grow up—or even go through life—dragging the chains their parents have riveted around their ankles. Chains of displaced ambitions, chains of unrealized dreams, chains of hobbies or activities that the parents enjoy and want their children to embrace and are upset or baffled or angry when they don't.

It's a subtle and insidious thing, this business of trying to mold or influence children to be what *you* want them to be. If a father has been a reasonably good athlete—say—or a mother a reasonably popular party girl, it seems quite natural to hope and expect that son or daughter will follow right along, or even surpass the parental model. Not only that, you tell yourself that common interests are the best way to bridge the generation gap. If mother and daughter both love to dance, if father and son share a love of fishing, what great and wonderful togetherness there will be!

Sometimes it works out like that. But sometimes it doesn't. Every child must go through the phase of rejecting the parent-model, shaking off those inherited values, trying to stand on his or her own feet. If parental pressure is too strong, or if the emerging adolescent personality is too weak, then these deadly chains may lock tight around the ankles and be dragged, with smoldering resentment or hidden fury, for years or maybe forever.

Somehow the parent must learn to say, not, "Be like me," but, "Be yourself, and let me help."

It's not an easy thing to do.

First Hunt

His father said, "All set, boy?" and Jeremy nodded quickly, picking up his gun with awkward mittened hands. His father pushed open the door and they went out into the freezing dawn together, leaving the snug security of the shack, the warmth of the kerosene stove, the companionable smell of bacon and coffee.

Not that Jeremy had eaten much breakfast. It had stuck in his throat, and his father, noticing this, had said, "Just a touch of buck fever, son; don't let it bother you." And he added, almost wistfully, "Wish I were fourteen again, getting ready to shoot my first duck. You're luckier than you realize, Jerry boy."

They stood for a moment in front of the shack, their breaths white in the icy air. Ahead of them was only flatness; not a house, not a tree, nothing but the vast expanse of marsh and water and sky. Ordinarily Jeremy would have been pleased by the bleak arrangements of black and gray and silver that met his eye. Ordinarily he would have asked his father to wait while he fussed around with his camera, trying to record these impressions on film. But not this morning. This was the morning, solemn and sacred, when he was to be initiated at last into the mystic rites of duck shooting.

This was the morning. And he hated it, had hated the whole idea ever since his father had bought him a gun, had taught him to shoot clay pigeons, had promised him a trip to this island in the bay where the point shooting was the finest in the state.

He hated it, but he was determined to go through with it. He loved his father, wanted more than anything in the world his approval and admiration. If only he could conduct himself properly this morning, he knew that he would get it.

Plodding now across the marshland, he remembered what his father had said to his mother after the first shotgun lesson: "You know, Martha, Jerry's got the makings of a fine wing shot. He's got coordination and timing. And—the kind of nerve it takes, too."

They came to the blind, a narrow, camouflaged pit facing the bay. In it was a bench, a shelf for shotgun shells, nothing else. Jeremy sat down tensely, waited while his father waded out with an armful of decoys. Light was pouring into the sky, now. Far down the bay a string of ducks went by, etched against the sunrise. Watching them, Jeremy felt his stomach contract.

To ease the sense of dread that was oppressing him, he picked up his camera and took a picture of his father silhouetted blackly against the quicksilver water. Then it occurred to him that this might not be the thing to do. He put the camera hastily on the shelf in front of him, picked up his gun again.

His father came back and dropped down beside him, boots dripping, hands blue with cold. "Better load up. Sometimes they're on top of you before you know it." He watched Jeremy break his gun, insert the shells, close it again. "I'll let you shoot first," he said, "and back you up if necessary." He loaded his own gun, closed it with a metallic snap. "You know," he said, happily, "I've been waiting a long time for this day. Just the two of us, out here on the marshes. We—"

He broke off, leaning forward, eyes narrowed. "There's a small flight now, headed this way. Four, no, five. Blacks, I think. They'll come in from left to right, against the wind, if they give us a shot at all. Keep your head down. I'll give you the word."

Jeremy kept his head down. Behind them the sun had cleared the horizon, now, flooding the marshes with tawny light. He could see everything with an almost unbearable clarity: his father's face, tense and eager, the faint white rime of frost on the gun barrels. His heart was thudding wildly. *No*, he prayed, *don't let them come. Make them stay away, please!*

But they kept coming. "Four blacks," his father said in a whisper. "One mallard. Keep still!"

Jeremy kept still. High above them, thin and sweet, he heard the pulsing whistle of wings as the flight went over, swung wide, began to circle. "Get set," Jeremy's father breathed. "They're coming."

In they came, gliding down the sunlit aisles of space, heads raised alertly, wings set in a proud curve. The mallard was leading; light flashed from the iridescent feathers around his neck and glinted on his ruddy breast. Down dropped his bright orange feet, reaching for the steel-colored water. Closer, closer . . .

"Now!" cried Jeremy's father in an explosive roar. He was on his feet, gun ready. "Take him! Take the leader!"

Jeremy felt his body obey. He stood up, leaned into the gun the way his father had taught him. He felt the stock cold against his cheek, saw the twin muzzles rise. Under his finger the trigger curved, smooth and final and deadly.

In the same instant, the ducks saw the gunners and flared wildly. Up went the mallard as if jerked by an invisible string. For a fraction of a second he hung there, poised against the wind and sun, balanced between life and death. *Now*, said something sharply in Jeremy's brain, *now!* And he waited for the slam of the explosion.

But it didn't come. Up went the mallard, higher still, until suddenly he tipped a wing, caught the full force of the wind, and whirled away, out of range, out of danger, out of sight.

There was no sound, then, except the faint rustle of the grasses. Jeremy stood there, gripping his gun.

"Well," his father said at last, "what happened?"

The boy did not answer. His lips were trembling.

His father said, in the same controlled voice, "Why didn't you shoot?"

Jeremy thumbed back the safety catch. He stood the gun carefully in the corner of the blind. "Because they were so alive," he said, and burst into tears.

He sat on the rough bench, face buried in his hands, and wept. All hope he had had of pleasing his father was gone. He had had his chance, and he had failed.

Beside him his father crouched suddenly. "Here comes a single. Looks like a pintail. Let's try again."

Jeremy did not lower his hands. "It's no use, Dad, I can't."

"Hurry," his father said roughly. "You'll miss him altogether. Here!"

Cold metal touched Jeremy. He looked up, unbelieving. His father had taken the camera out of its case, was offering it to him. "Quick, here he comes. He won't hang around all day!"

In swept the single, a big pintail drake driving low across the water, skidding right into the decoys. Jeremy's father clapped his hands together, a sound like a pistol shot. The splendid bird soared up; the pressure of his wings sent him twelve feet. One instant he was there, not thirty yards away, feet retracted, head raised, wings flailing, white breast gleaming. The next he was gone, whistling like a feathered bullet downwind.

Jeremy lowered the camera. "I got him!" His face was radiant. "I *got* him!"

"Did you?" His father's hand touched his shoulder briefly. "That's good. There'll be others along soon; you can get all sorts of shots." He hesitated, looking at his son, and Jeremy saw that there was no disappointment in his eyes, only pride and sympathy and love. "It's okay, son. I'll always love shooting. But that doesn't mean you have to. Sometimes, it takes just as much courage not to do a thing as to do it. Think you could teach me how to work that gadget?"

"Teach you?" Jeremy felt as if his heart would burst with happiness. "Gosh, Dad, there's nothing to it. It's easy, really it is. Look here, let me show you . . ."

XVI

When you look around and find that you have innumerable daughters, as I do, it's hard to know which one to choose as a model when you need a teenage character for a story. So I invented a composite named Christabel and used her with reasonable success over a period of years.

Christabel was usually intensely preoccupied with the opposite sex, and usually the interest was mutual. In this case she got mixed up with a couple of archangels, one fallen and one not. I have a notion that some readers never knew who Luce and Michael really were at all.

But then, neither did Christabel.

Christabel

Oh, what a girl was Christabel the summer she was nineteen! She had smoky red hair and green eyes that slanted a bit and a bikini that on anyone else might have led to police action. When she walked down the beach all the sea gulls—the he gulls, anyway—uttered plaintive cries, and it was said the more enterprising fish arranged themselves in rows just to see her pass by.

Christabel had no major vices, but her hobby was twisting masculine hearts into shapes resembling pretzels. Her father warned her she would get into trouble doing this. He was quite right.

The trouble began, stealthily enough, on a Monday morning. Christabel came out of her summer resort hotel feeling simply wonderful. She ran down to the water, plunged in, and swam out fifty yards or so. But then she couldn't get back. She swam and swam, and got absolutely nowhere. It was very exasperating.

At last the black-haired young man in the lifeguard's chair, who had been watching with amusement, swam out, put his arm around Christabel and brought her, damp and faintly puzzled, back to land. As he carried her up the beach— not that she needed carrying—he asked her for a date that evening.

"But I don't even know you," said Christabel demurely.

"Just call me Luce," said the young man. His bronzed arms were very strong; his dark eyes very admiring. He put her down, and Christabel realized she had been very warm and comfortable.

"I really shouldn't," she murmured. "I already have a date. It wouldn't be fair to break it, do you think?"

"Don't ask me," said Luce. "I'm no expert on morality."

Christabel sighed. "All right; I'll break it."

It was quite a morning for Christabel. On her way down to lunch she caught her heel in a worn bit of hotel carpet and plunged straight into the arms of another young man, tall, blond, and extremely handsome. His name, it seemed, was Michael; he had just registered at the desk. When he had made sure that Christabel was not hurt, he too asked her, very politely, for a date that night.

"I'm afraid," said Christabel, "I already have one." She looked up through long lashes. "Would it be fair to break it?"

"Certainly not," said Michael firmly. "What about tomorrow?"

Christabel mentally broke the date she had had for Tuesday night. "Why," she said sweetly, "I think that could be arranged!"

She went thoughtfully into the dining room, where her waiter sprang forward, tripping over his own feet. He was a large, rather clumsy fellow earning a few dollars by waiting on tables. In the fall, he would go back to college. He was so much in love with Christabel that he was constantly dropping dishes. The headwaiter always referred to him as That Oaf.

Christabel had a fine time with Luce that night. He was superb on the dance floor, especially in the more torrid rumbas. The only trouble was, Christabel found she grew unaccountably warm while dancing with him. So she suggested a moonlight walk.

Luce agreed with alacrity. But when, in the shadow of a convenient dune, he tried to draw her to him, she pushed him gently away. "I really am fond of you, Luce," she murmured, "but . . ."

"But what?" asked the hot-eyed young man.

"But I have the queerest feeling that there's something a little—well—wicked about you. I can't abide wickedness, really. If we're to go on seeing each other, I'm afraid you'll have to reform."

Luce looked into the slanting green eyes and felt himself grow dizzy, an unfamiliar sensation. "Reform?" he said doubtfully. "I'm not sure that I . . ."

Christabel reached up and straightened his tie. "Of course you can! It's much easier to be good than bad. You'll see." She patted his dark cheek; it felt cooler already.

"Gosh," said Luce weakly, "if you feel *that* way . . ."

"I do," she said firmly. "Now let's go back to the dance."

The next night, Christabel had her date with Michael. He was also a good dancer, in a somewhat stately way. But he was rather scornful of the orchestra. "I know a fellow," he said. "Boy, can he play the trumpet! You ought to hear him." He looked thoughtful. "Maybe you will."

Eventually he also took Christabel out on the beach. Not to try to kiss her, or anything like that. To warn her about Luce. "I think it's my duty to tell you that he's no good. In fact, he's an absolute fiend!"

"How do you know?" asked Christabel, much interested.

"I knew him," said Michael darkly, "when."

"You're sweet, Michael," said Christabel, "to worry about me. But don't you think perhaps you're a mite *too* proper? I mean, there's nothing wrong with a kiss or two, is there?" She looked into his eyes, and *he* felt a great dizziness seize him.

"Well—uh—no," he stammered. "I guess not. Not really."

"Why," said Christabel softly, "don't you kiss me, then?" And, "Oh," she said a moment later, "did you see that falling star?"

Christabel went on seeing Luce and Michael alternately the rest of the week. By the time Saturday night came around, you'd hardly have known either of them. Christabel was very pleased. She asked them both to take her to the dance.

Since she was a young lady who took her time about dressing, it happened that Luce and Michael met each other pacing nervously near the elevator. Luce spoke first. "You've changed," he said, "but you don't fool me. I know you!"

"I know you too," snapped Michael, whose temper was no longer exactly angelic. "You—you renegade! What do you think they're going to say to you when you get home?"

"That," said Luce, "is a question you should ask yourself."

"I have," said Michael, grinding his teeth. "The answer is, they never should have sent me to protect her from you in the first place. I'm not the—er—person for the job."

"Look, Michael," Luce said. "I know we're not supposed to—uh—cooperate. But we're both in a bad spot."

"We sure are," said Michael glumly.

"If we change much more, neither of us will be good or bad. We'll just be in love. With Christabel."

"I know it," said Michael miserably. "I never knew a mortal soul like her."

"I have," said Luce, "a little suggestion." He looked furtively over his shoulder. "You have some—ah—unique powers, don't you? Well, so have I. Now, if just for once we pooled our—"

"The Oaf!" exclaimed Michael, reading his mind of course.

"Exactly! We'll make her fall in love with The Oaf. Then we can be ourselves again. We can even go home!"

"It's a deal!" cried Michael, and before they knew what they were doing, they were shaking hands. . . .

"And *that*, children," said the storyteller, "is how your mother happened to marry me, since I am none other than—"

"The Oaf!" they squealed in unison.

"Off to bed now," he said, and patted their small pajama'd bottoms. He looked across the room at the girl with the green eyes and the smoky red hair. "Fairly accurate version, wasn't it, dear?"

"Not very," said Christabel. "I was in love with you all the time. You oaf!"

XVII

One reason I think the short story is far from dead is the number of people who try to write them. In colleges, I'm told, creative writing courses flourish. Every summer writers' conferences attended by thousands of eager note takers spring up all over the land. The magazine I once worked for used to conduct two national writing contests, one for adults, one for high-school students. Each one attracted between three and four thousand manuscripts, all of which were faithfully read. Maybe, with luck, six or eight were publishable.

The magazine also conducted a writers' workshop that lasted a week and brought together a dozen or so writers whose manuscripts, submitted in the adult contest, showed promise. I used to give talks at these gatherings, plagued by a faint sense of guilt because I wasn't sure then—and I'm not sure now—that writing really can be *taught*. Oh, you can point out things to do or not to do. But unless the listener has a built-in sense of the dramatic, a natural ear for words, an ability to think fairly clearly, the persistence of a horsefly and the tenacity of a crocodile, you are probably wasting your time. Oh, yes, the listener should also have a low boring point. A writer has to be able to bore himself (and know it) a fraction of a moment before he bores the reader, and take remedial action. Otherwise, he's doomed.

Beginning writers make understandable mistakes. They're seldom content to write the way they talk—the best way to start out—so they sit down all tensed up and try to Write with a capital W. This self-conscious approach seldom works. Sometimes they offer you a Slice of Life, carefully described. The trouble with this is that life in thin slices seldom makes a point, which is precisely what the reader wants the story to do—make a valid point.

There's no foolproof formula for short-story writing. Even if someone does try to set up neat little rules, a story will come along and brush them aside. In "The Sea Devil," for example, the protagonist has no name; the manuals would say he should have one. The manuals say there should be dialogue; there's not a line of it. They say you need several characters; there's only one. Yet the story has been reprinted far more often than any other in this book.

In general, if you're ever seized with an urge to try this crazy business, there are a few things to remember. In most cases, a story needs an appealing central character for the reader to focus on and identify with. This character should come into the story at Point *A* with some kind of *minus*—a problem, a fear, a threat, a danger, a broken relationship—and leave it at Point *Z* with a *plus*, a problem solved, a danger evaded, an objective gained, a relationship healed. In between Point *A* and Point *Z* there should be increasing complication, mounting suspense, and finally a logical and believable Point of Resolution where things get straightened out. Unless they're straightened out, the reader is going to feel dissatisfied, even cheated.

Those are the basic ingredients and they don't vary much, regardless of setting or time frame. If you look carefully, you'll recognize them in almost any story, even a legend set in thirteenth-century Italy.

The First Creche

More than seven hundred years ago in the village of Greccio in Italy there lived a man who was at war with God. His name was Luigi, and he had his reasons.

He was a strong man, black-eyed, hot-tempered, with wonderful sensitive hands. From childhood, he had had the gift of shaping wood into marvelous imitations of life. And for a long time, he accepted this talent with gratitude, as a sign of God's favor. But the day came when Luigi cursed heaven. It was the day he learned that his daughter—his only child—was blind.

She had seemed perfect when she was born: blonde and blue-eyed like her mother. But when it became apparent that the child would never see, the wood-carver of Greccio seemed to go mad.

He went no more to the little church on the hill. He refused to allow prayers in his house. His child had been called Maria, after the mother of Jesus. He changed her name to Rosa.

His wife pleaded in vain; nothing could move him. "I will have nothing to do," he said, "with a God who condemns innocent children to darkness." To an artist, blindness is like a sentence of death.

Then in mid-December, in the year 1207, a mule train came through Greccio. Among the treasures for sale was a magnificent piece of ivory. As soon as he saw it, Luigi had the thought that he would carve it into a doll—a *bambino*—for his little girl.

In three days it was finished. Life-sized, smiling, with tiny arms outstretched, the ivory *bambino* seemed almost to breathe. Luigi told no one about it except his wife, and he told her only because he wanted her to make some clothes for the doll.

Meantime, in the village, everyone was talking about the young friar who had come to Greccio from a neighboring town to preach in the little church. No one could say exactly what it was about his preaching, but people who heard him came away with an extraordinary sense of peace, as if all the anger and pain of living had been lifted from their hearts.

Luigi's wife heard the young friar preach, and she begged her husband to come to the church with her. But Luigi shook his head. "When this God of yours shows me that he can cure blindness, then I will believe in him."

He would not let his wife take Rosa, either. But she wanted desperately to bring her child into some sort of contact with the love and warmth that seemed to flow from the young friar. And on Christmas Eve, suddenly, she thought of a way.

When by chance Luigi went into his workshop, his shout of fury brought the servants running. The ivory *bambino* was gone. From a terrified maid, Luigi learned that his wife had taken it to the church to have it blessed.

Out into the street stalked Luigi, black anger in his heart. Up the hill he went through the pale December sunlight toward the little church. But before he could reach the door, a cavalcade swept up the hill, three young nobles, richly dressed, then half a dozen mounted servants, and finally two carts loaded with farm animals: sheep, goats, oxen, a donkey.

The riders pulled up at the church door with a chorus of shouts. A young man in a purple cloak sprang down.

"Francesco!" he shouted. "Francesco Bernardone! We got your message and we are here!"

Luigi spoke roughly to one of the servants. "Who is this Francesco Bernardone that you seek here in Greccio?"

The servant pointed. "That is he—the friar."

The church door had opened, and a slender, brown-clad figure had come out. "Welcome my friends," he said, smiling, "and God's peace be upon you all."

The young man in the purple cloak swept his arm in a wide gesture. "We've brought the animals, just as you said. But really, Francesco, how much longer are you going to play this farce?"

Luigi tightened his hold on the servant's shoulder. "Who is this man?"

The servant shrugged despairingly. "In Assisi, until not long ago, he was my master's friend and drinking companion.

Now, they say, he preaches the word of God. It is very strange."

Other servants were unloading the carts, where the frightened animals reared and plunged. "A moment, please," the friar said. He walked over to the nearest cart and laid his hand on the donkey's back. "Be calm, there, Brother Ass. And you, Sister Sheep, do not baa so pitifully." And even as he spoke, the animals grew calm and still.

A hush seemed to fall upon the people who had gathered. In this sudden quiet, the friar said to the young man in the purple cloak. "Come into the church, Lorenzo. I want to show you my manger scene."

The young man said in a low voice, "I am not a true believer, Francesco. You know that."

"All the more reason for coming," the little friar said. He turned and went back into the church, and all the animals followed him, and the people, too. Even Luigi.

Inside the church, candles burned dimly. Near the altar was a rude shelter, made of green boughs, and in the shelter was a manger. Luigi could not see into the manger, but he knew what it contained, for a woman was kneeling near it, her face beautiful in the candlelight. The woman was his wife.

Without being led, without being driven, the animals grouped themselves around the manger. Then the little friar stood up on the steps of the altar.

"I was going to read you the Christmas story from the gospel," he said. "But my nativity scene makes me so happy that I am going to sing it to you."

No one who heard it ever forgot the sweetness of his song. He told the ageless story of the angels and the shepherds, of the coming of the Wise Men. Even the animals seemed to be listening, as if they too could understand the words. And Luigi was prepared to believe that they could, because an even greater miracle was taking place within himself. The bitterness and the anger were fading from his heart.

Nor was his the only heart that was being changed, for when at last the music ended, the young man in the purple cloak moved forward. From around his neck he took a chain of gold and put it beside the manger. And after him his companions came and put down gifts, one a ring, the other a jeweled dagger.

Luigi felt a touch on his arm. Looking around, he saw the little friar smiling at him.

"You wondered if God could cure blindness," the friar said. "Well, we are watching him do it, are we not?"

Luigi did not answer, for there was a tightness in his throat. He could see the villagers crowding forward to look into the manger and the awe and wonder in their faces as they gazed upon his handiwork. Afterward, there were those who swore that the ivory *bambino* stirred and smiled and lifted his arms to them. But this, no doubt, was the flickering candlelight.

Then the friar said, "Please thank your daughter for the loan of her Christmas present. And now you may take it back."

Luigi shook his head. "It is where it belongs. Let it stay."

The friar said, "Tomorrow is Christmas. Your little girl would be disappointed."

"No," said Luigi, "I will make her another *bambino*. I will work all night. I will carve her a whole nativity scene, just like yours, so that Ro—I mean Maria—will have Christmas at her fingertips whenever she wants it."

So Luigi went home, leaving the ivory *bambino* with Saint Francis of Assisi in what, according to legend, was the first actual creche. Hand in hand with his wife, he walked back down the hill. And he worked all night with gratitude in his heart because he knew that in his house blindness had indeed been cured—not his daughter's, but his own.

XVIII

Strange, isn't it, when you look back through the years, how much innocence you seem to see. *Innocence* in the basic meaning of the word: "unacquainted with evil." You seem to see it in so many areas of living. Boy-girl relationships, for example. Twenty-five or thirty years ago they weren't exactly platonic (they never were), but they weren't harsh or crude or exploitative either.

The whole culture was different then. Movies were simplistic, almost naive. Musical comedies were mostly tuneful nonsense. Books were nonexplicit. Even the theatre was fairly restrained.

It all changed drastically in the last decade or two, maybe male-female relationships most of all. It's hard to say exactly why. Maybe in the name of honesty and candor and freedom from hypocrisy—good motives all—we opened the door first to casual sex and then to indiscriminate sex and finally to pornography with all its dreary camp followers. Most of us watched in troubled silence, not knowing what to do about it. A sense of outrage is a fragile thing; it crumbles under a succession of shocks until finally it vanishes, leaving us accepting almost automatically what once we would have despised.

One of the casualties along the way was that shimmering soap bubble known as romance. There used to be a genuine demand for it, and perhaps there still is, because when a faint nostalgic echo of it comes along today, it seems to me that people are less inclined to jeer or sneer than they were—oh, say ten years ago.

No, the main reaction now is one of incredulity that such gentle and structured and mannered times could ever really have existed. If you listen carefully, you can hear a touch of wistfulness there too, almost as if a faint awareness were beginning to stir, an awareness that those who shut romance out of their lives are missing something. Something very important.

"Tell me," a young girl says wonderingly, "did they really dance waltzes in those days? In long dresses, with flowers in their hair? Was there really something called a stag line? Did unattached men really cut in?"

Why, yes, Virginia, they really did. And some day—who knows—maybe, they'll do it again.

The Bargain

He stood in the stag line at some country club or other, watching the dancers circle the floor in a dreamy waltz. Outside, the night was warm and still; along the moon-silvered fairways the katydids sang their midsummer song.

He stood there, a little taller than the rest, trying to decide honestly which was the prettiest girl on the floor. It was a pleasant choice, but not an easy one. In the dim light, white shoulders gleaming, faces rapt, long dresses whispering, they were all lovely. Or so it seemed.

His host nudged him as a tall blonde, cool and delicious in silver lamé, swirled past. "Want an introduction?"

He shook his head. "Never use 'em, thanks."

A redhead in green danced past; then a little brunette with a gardenia in her hair. For several minutes he watched them as they drifted like butterflies from one partner to another. The blonde was beautiful, certainly; but she was also a little aloof. The redhead . . . no. The brunette danced close to her partners, flame-colored dress molded to her figure, eyes half-closed, lashes dark against her cheek.

Abruptly he made up his mind. He stepped into the eddying sea of faces, tapped the brunette's partner on the shoulder. She came into his arms without looking at him, and the scent of gardenia, warm and fragrant, came with her. When she did glance up, her eyes were like damp violets. They were also faintly hostile.

"Don't look so annoyed," he said. "We've met, I'm sure. Several incarnations ago, probably."

She did not answer. They danced for a moment in silence. She was as light on her feet as a falling leaf. The top of her head came just to his chin.

"You don't seem convinced," he said finally. He saw someone preparing to cut in, and he added hastily. "Perhaps if you'll come out on the veranda with me, I'll be able to refresh your memory."

She stopped dancing. "My memory is perfect," she said. But she went with him.

They stepped out onto the white-railed veranda where cigarettes glowed in the semidarkness. The girl paused by the railing, but the man took her arm and drew her gently down the steps and along the path that led to the tennis courts. She did not resist, but she said coolly, "You seem to know your way around here pretty well."

He laughed. "Instinct," he said. "Besides, I have a favor to ask which you couldn't possibly grant on the veranda."

"Indeed?" she said. "I thought you brought me out here to refresh my memory?"

"I'm afraid," he told her, "that I brought you out here because I want to kiss you."

"Well!" she said. Her eyes were wide in the moonlight.

"You sound almost desperate. Won't anyone here take pity on a poor stranger? Or have you tried them all?"

He frowned. "You sound like my wife," he said.

If she was startled, she did not show it. "Don't tell me your wife misunderstands you," she murmured.

"On the contrary," he said, "she understands me very well. She knows I have a weakness for pretty girls. So tonight, when I suggested that she give me her permission in advance to kiss the prettiest one I could find, she agreed. Oh, she was a bit surly about it, but she agreed. One kiss. Provided, of course, the lady is willing." He paused. "And is she?"

She was smiling a little, now. "You think I'm the prettiest one?"

"Lady," he said, "you are."

As he said it, they passed under the shadow of a lilac bush, and he leaned forward hopefully. But she drew back.

"What about your poor wife?" she asked. "What does she get out of this—this—experiment?"

"Oh," he told her, "she can kiss any man she wants. Just once. That's part of the bargain."

She looked at him. "Tell me," she said, "does your wife have to inform her—victim—that she is married too?"

"No," he said, "she doesn't. But she does have to take off her wedding ring before she kisses him. I was quite firm about that."

The girl looked down at her own hands, pale in the moonlight. "Are you quite sure you want to share this—ah—extramarital kiss with me? After all, you're allowed only one. Weren't there any other girls that took your fancy?"

"There was a blonde," he admitted candidly. "She was beautiful. But you were the prettiest. That was the bargain."

She turned to him suddenly and put her arms around his neck. He bent his head. Around them the katydids shrilled louder than ever, but the universe stood still. Slowly, reluctantly, they drew apart. They looked at each other.

"Thank you," he said finally.

"Thank *you*," she answered gravely. "Shall we go back in, now?"

"I think not," he said. "I have a better idea." He kissed her again. "Put your ring back on," he said. "We're going home."

XIX

It says something about us human beings—something good, I think—that we're always trying to improve our performance. If you're a student, it's better grades. If you're a cook, it's a better casserole. If you're an architect, it's a better building. If you're a poet, it's a better poem. Always a reach for a degree of excellence never quite obtainable.

The struggle toward perfection seems to get harder as you come closer. But I wonder sometimes, if you did succeed in touching it, whether everything might suddenly become effortless. The joy of doing whatever you were doing perfectly, I think, might transcend the struggle so completely that the struggle itself would disappear.

An odd idea, perhaps. But I remember very distinctly where it came from. It came from something that happened years ago when I was an oarsman at college.

Anyone who has been a member of an eight-oared crew will tell you that rowing may well be the most demanding of sports. It stretches your endurance to the absolute bone-cracking limit. It calls for exquisite timing. It's based on total teamwork: A single mistake by one member of the crew can lose the race for the other seven members—eight, if you count the coxswain. It's a sport that demands complete coordination, mental and physical, from everyone in the boat.

Such coordination comes only from endless practice. There's an old saying among oarsmen: "Mileage makes champions." The more miles a crew rows together, the closer it comes to the complete unity, the absolute oneness, that it is always seeking.

It was early spring on the Housatonic, Connecticut's loveliest river; the trees were just beginning to show feathers of green. We had rowed several miles upstream from the boathouse on an ordinary practice run, trailed as usual by the white coaching launch. It was one of those days when nothing seemed to please the hooded figure with the megaphone in the bow of the launch. Sarcasm was the lash our coach used sometimes to sting us into better performance. But today he apparently judged our performance too dismal to merit any comment at all. Finally, miles from home, he announced that he couldn't bear to look at us any longer. Whereupon he turned the launch around and sped away downstream, leaving us there.

It was a surly crew that started the long row back. You could almost hear the mutinous thoughts running through every head. *So we aren't much good. So what? So who cares about this crazy sport anyway? Only an idiot would choose to spend his time like this.* And so on.

By now it was almost dark. The trees were massed shadows along the tranquil river; the sunset had faded; the first stars were beginning to show through. We slogged along morosely at about twenty-two strokes per minute, far below racing speed. The shell felt heavy; every stroke was an effort.

But suddenly an extraordinary thing happened; everything changed. Perhaps because we *weren't* trying, perhaps because we *didn't* care, the whole crew came together. As if a master conductor were orchestrating it, the ragged timing became flawless. The friction of the water vanished; at every stroke the shell seemed to skim along on quicksilver. The pressure on the oar blades seemed to disappear; they were like feathers drawing long smooth lines through empty air. Everything was effortless: no strain, no stress, just perfect rhythm, pure exhilaration, astonished joy. There was no sound except the hiss of water under our sliding seats, and the muffled double thump of eight oars striking the river at precisely the same split second and releasing it again with the same marvelous precision, and the hollow thunk of water falling back into the holes made by the blades. It wasn't like rowing; it was like flying. And all of us knew it.

How long it lasted, I don't know. Perhaps a half mile. Maybe a mile. I couldn't account for it then—none of us could—and I can't account for it now. But I never forgot it, or the lesson it seemed to teach: that if you do something really right, there is no fatigue, no strain, no effort in it at all because you are in harmony with something that simply brushes those things away.

I think those great rhythms and patterns underlie all reality. Some are physical. Some are ethical. Here's a story about a doctor's struggle to bring himself into alignment with a code of conduct that something inside of him knew was right.

Dr. Marlowe's Dilemma

In the basement of the great hospital was a cafeteria where members of the staff could eat quickly and conveniently, absenting themselves only briefly from the vast, organized program of healing, the never-ending struggle against the dark legions of death.

It was past the dinner hour now, but the place was still crowded. All the tables were filled, or partly filled, and young Dr. Marlowe hesitated, holding his tray with both hands.

The harsh overhead lights struck down sharply, burnishing his hair and making his fine-drawn face look paler than it actually was. He said, over his shoulder, "Couple of seats over there, Alan."

Dr. Alan Gillespie deftly twitched a spoon from the container of silverware. He was about the same age as Marlowe, but he looked older, a stocky, broad-shouldered man with a kind of terrier assurance about him. He had been wearing his reflector, that badge of the ear-nose-and-throat specialist, and the strap had left an inch-wide mark across his forehead just above his dark eyes.

"Lead on," he said. "I'm right with you. But honestly, Jim. I don't understand—"

"Skip it, will you Alan?" Jim Marlowe moved forward, threading his way through the white-clad figures until he came to a table for four set close to the wall. Two of the chairs were occupied by nurses who gave the doctors respectful smiles and made room with a whisper of starched skirts.

Gillespie set his tray down decisively. "I won't skip it! I'd give my eyeteeth to be doing that operation in the morning. So would Gray, so would Murchison. Old Pollard picks you. That's all right; you're a better surgeon than the rest of us. Everybody knows that, and nobody resents it. But instead of being pleased and excited, you act as if—"

"Look, Alan," Marlowe said, "how *I* feel is my own business, isn't it?"

"Not really, no! A case like this one only comes along once in a blue moon. How the surgery is handled makes a lot of difference to all of us. Everybody'll be watching, you know. I bet the amphitheater's jammed. If—"

"I know, I know!" Marlowe pulled the sugar toward him. His long fingers, rock steady, filled a spoon to the last grain, emptied it precisely into the steaming coffee.

"Well, what's bothering you, then?" Gillespie's voice was like a terrier's bark, abrupt and challenging. "Not getting stage fright, are you?"

"No! It's just that the old man is going to die anyway. The thing's gone too far. I can't save him. Nobody can."

Gillespie rubbed the back of his hand across his chin, his eyes thoughtful. "You can't cure him, no. But you may prolong his life a bit. That's what Pollard expects you to do. That and learn."

"Why prolong his life when it'll just prolong his suffering? The poor old boy has no relatives, no friends, even. Why operate at all? Why not just give him his sedatives and let him die in peace?"

"Why operate?" Gillespie's dark eyebrows climbed almost to the fading mark of the reflector on his forehead. "Why, man, the things you'll learn in that one operation are priceless, absolutely priceless! Talk about radical surgery! Why, you'll have to—"

"I know what I'll have to do," Marlowe said grimly. He had a sudden prevision of himself, robed and masked, standing under the glaring lights. Cancer of the sinuses, extremely advanced.

Again the flash of anger lanced through him. "Look, Alan, I've done dozens of operations. But always trying to save a life, or reduce pain, or prevent suffering. I've never done one where I felt I couldn't really help the patient, where the motive was partly selfish, to learn something at the expense of—"

"But man, it's *not* selfish." Gillespie cried. "If you prolong life even twenty-four hours, that's justification in itself! Besides, you're a doctor, aren't you? An instrument of healing, right? Well, after this job you'll be a better doctor, a more effective instrument of healing. Maybe you can't cure Old Man Harris, but by operating on him you'll learn things that will enable you to save other lives."

He took a furious gulp of his coffee and plunged on. "You know what old Pollard keeps saying: 'In surgery, there's no substitute for experience.' Well, that's true. If it weren't, we could learn all we need to know in the dissecting room where there's no gamble because there are no stakes! In this case, you've got to take half the patient's face away and still keep his heart beating. It's a terrific problem and a terrific challenge!"

One of the nurses finished her dessert, eased back her chair with a murmured, "Excuse me," and left the table.

Marlowe pushed his coffee away untouched. "I can't help wondering," he said wearily, "whether surgery would be scheduled for tomorrow if the old man weren't a charity patient. If he were some millionaire, or even a private patient."

"If he were a private patient," Gillespie said with conviction, "he wouldn't be in such awful shape. He'd have done something about his condition long ago. But he's just a poor old derelict who let the thing go too far."

He drained his cup and set it down. "I've got to run. The lady's a redhead, and she doesn't like to be kept waiting." He reached out and cuffed Marlowe affectionately. "You ought to get yourself a girl, Jim. You sit around and think too much. Never mind; I'll be in the front row tomorrow morning, cheering for you. See you then."

He moved away with his dancing terrier gait. Marlowe watched him go, his eyes somber and a little envious. Slowly he drew his coffee cup toward him, raised it—and for the first time glanced at the nurse sitting opposite.

The smooth chestnut hair under the immaculate cap, the eyes neither brown nor gray but some indefinable color between, the gentle mouth, the hint of stubbornness in the chin—these things seemed familiar to him, and he said to her, smiling a little, "Haven't I seen you before?"

She nodded. "Several times, Dr. Marlowe."

He wrinkled his forehead, trying to remember. "In one of the wards, wasn't it? Let's see, you're Miss . . . Miss . . ."

"Andrews. This week I'm on night duty in Ward 12." She glanced at her watch. "I'm due there in exactly three minutes."

"Ward 12? That's where Old Man Harris is!"

She nodded, reaching for her check.

"Then you're familiar with the case—the one Dr. Gillespie and I were talking about!"

She nodded again, saying nothing; this reticence was proper, he knew, but suddenly the pressure inside him demanded some kind of release. "You heard the discussion," he said, harshly. "Everything Gillespie said was true! Then why do I feel this way, as if—as if something were missing, something terribly important, something . . ." He broke off with a helpless gesture.

She said in a low, hesitant voice, "Something *is* missing."

He had been hoping for reassurance, not this confirmation of his own misgivings. "What is it, then?"

She shook her head and stood up quickly, as if she wanted to get away from him and the problem he represented.

"Wait a minute," he said sharply. "Tell me what's missing."

She looked down at him for a long moment. "The consent of the patient," she said, and turned away.

He sat there, feeling something tighten inside him, some nameless emotion that crystalized suddenly into hot resentment. Consent of the patient—why, that was preposterous! They already had Old Man Harris' consent, had it in writing. Every patient facing surgery had to sign a release giving full permission. Or some close relative had to sign it. She knew that perfectly well. What was she talking about?

He watched her go up to the cashier, pay her bill, go out. Under the edge of the table he clenched his fist slowly. Consent of the patient, indeed. Suppose in every case of major surgery the doctor had to give the patient a complete blueprint of cause and effect, of possibility and probability, of why and wherefore. The results would be chaotic!

The doctor had the facts, the knowledge, and consequently the responsibility. He had to be the sole judge, often, of what was the best thing to do.

A sudden impulse came to him to follow this nurse, explain these things, wring from her an admission that they were so. Make her understand, at least, that the decision to operate had not been his. Convince her that it had been an assignment that could not be shirked or avoided, and in convincing her banish the last of his own foolish misgivings and doubts.

He picked up his check, walked rapidly to the cashier's cage, paid it, went out into the corridor. As he rode up in the elevator, he noticed that his heart had begun to pound with a heavy, uneven rhythm. He knew the reason well enough: adrenaline, pouring unbidden into his bloodstream. And he knew the emotion that most often triggered such a reaction: It was fear. *What's the matter with you?* he said angrily to himself. *You're just doing your job. You have nothing to be afraid of . . .*

He pushed through the swinging doors that led to Ward 12. The nurses' alcove was empty. Miss Andrews, he knew, could be in any one of a dozen places, but the thought came to him instantly that she might be with Old Man Harris in the little room just off the ward where patients were placed the night before surgery. He walked quickly toward it, opened the door, went in.

Miss Andrews was not there, but Old Man Harris was. He lay quietly in the tall bed, big-knuckled hands resting on the white sheets, waiting. He was quite alone. Invisible, but all around him, much more noticeable in this narrow room than it had been in the open ward, was the sickly, unmistakable odor of dissolution, of decay.

"Hi, there, Doc," he said. Recognition flickered in his eyes. "They tell me you're the one's going to fix me up in the morning." He nodded slowly, as if quite content. "I sure am glad," the old voice said.

Jim Marlowe closed the door and set his shoulders against it, hearing the inner voice that he had tried to silence speak plainly now. *She's right,* said this inner voice, *that's exactly what's missing—the consent of the patient. Sure, the old man signed the release. Because he believes that the operation is essential. Because he thinks that it will help him, may even cure him. Because he has faith . . .*

The doctor felt the irregular pounding of his heart begin again, and this time he knew why he was afraid. If he told Old Man Harris the truth, the consequences to his own career might be most unfortunate.

Old Pollard did not like to have his decisions questioned. If permission for the operation were suddenly withdrawn, the reason would assuredly become known, and then . . .

"You look sort of worried, Doc. What's on your mind?"

Jim Marlowe found that his mouth was suddenly dry. He moved over and sat down on the edge of the bed. "Mr. Harris," he said, and his own voice sounded strange to him, "there are some things I'd like to say to you—before tomorrow morning."

He talked for five minutes, steadily, blotting his forehead now and then with his sleeve. He tried to be scrupulously fair. He pointed out that there might well be some benefit, however slight and temporary, from surgery. But he made no effort to conceal his opinion that in the end the surgeon would gain more from the operation than the patient.

Old Man Harris lay there, watching him, not saying a word. Even when Marlowe stopped talking, he said nothing for perhaps thirty seconds. Then, "Why'd you tell me all this, Doc?"

"Someone," Jim Marlowe said, "someone made me see that you had a right to know. You can still call off the whole deal, if you want to. But no one else can."

Silence sang in the little room; the seconds ticked away.

"Well, son," the old voice said at last, "from what you say, it can't do me no harm—I'm done for anyway. And maybe you'll learn something . . ." The old voice trailed off, then came back, suddenly strong. "All my life," said Old Man Harris, "all my life I've been pretty worthless, really. Would be sort of nice, wouldn't it, right at the end, if I could do some good?"

Outside, in the dim corridor, Jim Marlowe stood quietly for a moment, letting the tension drain out of him, feeling it replaced by a tremendous surge of confidence, an amazing sense of lightness and well-being. He walked quickly toward the swinging doors. Then he stopped.

Miss Andrews was sitting at the desk in the nurses' alcove, making entries on some patient's chart. Light from the hooded lamp, reflecting upward, outlined the column of her throat, gleamed on her chestnut hair. She glanced up; the tiny scratching of the fountain pen ceased.

He stopped in front of her. "I've been talking to Old Man Harris. I didn't ask for it, exactly—but he gave his consent."

She nodded gravely, as if what he had done did not surprise her, as if, indeed, she had known all along that he would do it. And this, too, added to his extraordinary sense of exhilaration and happiness.

He moved away from her, but at the swinging doors he looked back, wanting to see her again, to fix her face indelibly in his mind. "Good night, Miss Andrews. And—thank you."

She had turned and was watching him go. Her face was in shadow, now; he could not see it clearly. But he heard the warmth in her voice, and the pride.

"Sleep well, Doctor," she said.

XX

All of us have friends who have had trouble with alcohol.
It's a terrible affliction because it hurts so many people—not
just the victim but all the people around him. Especially
family. Most especially children.

Some alcoholics turn to Alcoholics Anonymous and find a
lifeline that saves them. Some—a few—manage to save
themselves. I knew a brilliant man in the publishing world
who stopped drinking by developing and using a kind of
mental trick. Every day, the first time alcohol came to his at-
tention in any form (an ad in the paper, a sign on a bill-
board, a mention on the radio, anything at all) he would stop
whatever he was doing and make himself relive, in all its hu-
miliating detail, the last binge he had gone on: the smashed
furniture, the weeping wife, the terrified children, the fight
with the police, the filth and vomit of the drunk tank at the
police station, the horrible morning after. Every single day
he made himself do this. And he never drank again.

But even after an alcoholic stops drinking, there are
bridges to be rebuilt. And that's not easy either.

The Long Road Back

The train had brought him swiftly, he had found the school
without difficulty, but now the headmistress said, looking at
him with troubled eyes, "You should have given us some
warning, Mr. Caldwell. I really don't think it's fair to Lisa to
have you—," she hesitated for a fraction of a second—, "to
have you just appear like this."

He twisted the brim of his rain-sodden hat, a slender man in
his mid-thirties, rather pale and ill at ease. "I know it's sud-
den," he said humbly, "and I thought of calling from the sta-
tion. But—well . . ." *Oh, can't you see*, a voice inside him was
imploring her, *can't you see that I was afraid to telephone? Afraid
that you wouldn't let me see her, or that you'd consult her mother and
she would refuse permission, or that . . .*

The clear eyes behind the rimless glasses were watching
him, weighing, judging, appraising. Dr. Bainbridge had
warned him about that. "You'll probably run into a certain
amount of distrust and suspicion at first, Caldwell. We've
done our best to make people on the outside realize that alco-
holism is a disease, not a moral problem. But . . ."

The headmistress said, "I honestly don't know how Lisa
feels about you, Mr. Caldwell. It's hard to tell, sometimes,
just what a ten-year-old is thinking. And, as you know, her
mother . . ."

She left the sentence unfinished, but he knew what she
meant. Grace was bitter, terribly bitter; she might have trans-
ferred some of her bitterness to the child. She was remarried
now, she had a new life of her own, but . . . He said, desper-
ately, hopefully, "Has Lisa been happy here?"

The headmistress smiled, looking suddenly much younger.
"I think all our children are happy, Mr. Caldwell. We try to
give them two things they need most: affection and disci-
pline." As if his question had helped her reach a decision, she
stood up, crossed the room, opened a door. "If you'll wait in
here, I'll have Lisa brought down for a few minutes."

He hesitated, feeling the familiar panic grip him, the fear of physical restraints that had come upon him during those first dreadful months in the hospital, the blind unreasoning terror at the thought of having a door close on him, of being shut in. Dr. Bainbridge had promised that some day this fear would leave him, as his other problems had left him. But it was still there. He said, "Would you mind if—if I left the door open a little?"

If she found this request strange, she did not show it. "Do whatever makes you feel most comfortable, Mr. Caldwell."

He went in, leaving the door slightly ajar. It was a long, narrow room, paneled in some dark wood, facing a courtyard where the November rain fell bleakly. The furniture was oak, solid and uncompromising. The room itself felt unused, dead. At the far end was another door, closed.

He put his hat down nervously on the polished surface of a table, then picked it up again. How would his own child feel about him after all these months? What would he say to her?

Unbidden, the scene rose up again in his mind, the scene he had tried so often to forget, the last scene, really, in which he had any clear memory of Lisa at all. It had been a hot summer night; the quarrel started—as so many had started—when he had objected to Grace's latest extravagance. And it had followed the grim, compulsive pattern: accusation, recrimination, fury where once there had been tenderness, ferocity where once there had been love. On and on, until he fled to the tavern that was almost a second home by now, drank and drank until the jagged splinters inside him lost their edges and reality faded and nothing mattered any more.

Then he had stumbled back to the apartment to find Grace waiting for him, to mock him, to jeer at what she called his weakness, to lash him with her tongue until a kind of madness came upon him. He had not offered violence to Grace; he had not even thought of touching her. But in his frenzy, his drunken frenzy, he had smashed furniture and mirrors, had ripped down curtains, had torn pictures from the wall. Until suddenly a door opened and Lisa was standing there. Lisa, with terror in her small face as she looked upon the madman who was her father. Lisa, who shrank away from him, weeping . . .

He took out a handkerchief and blotted his forehead. To

steady himself, he summoned up an image of Dr. Bainbridge's strong, patient face, made himself hear again the calm, unhurried voice that had reached down, down, down into the horrible pit where he had been lying: "You're in a state hospital, Caldwell . . . rehabilitation program for people like you . . . we're going to cure you, Caldwell . . . but it will take time . . . time . . ."

And then, later, when his mind was beginning to function again: "Your drinking wasn't caused by overwork, Caldwell, as you thought. Or by lack of will power, as your wife thought. Actually, the same set of reasons that made you work so hard made you drink too hard. It was insecurity, going far back into your childhood. Insecurity, plus marriage to a woman who failed to understand your needs when you needed her most. A woman—I can say this, now that she's divorced you—who was immature herself, and selfish, and cold. But that's all over and done with now. We're going to sort out things for you, untangle the knots, put you back in circulation . . ."

And finally, only this morning, "Well, Caldwell, this is a great day for both of us. You must never touch alcohol again, and I'm pretty sure you'll never want to. The main thing now is to find someone to care about, to work hard for—but not too hard!—lose yourself in trying to make someone else happy . . ."

Someone you care about . . .

The door at the far end of the room opened and Lisa came in. She stood quite still in her white blouse and dark blue skirt, facing him. She was taller than he had expected, and thinner. Her face was pale; her eyes looked enormous.

He took a step forward. "Hello—Lisa." The words sounded strained, awkward. So did his voice.

She put her back flat against the door, saying nothing to him. He stopped, feeling the hostility like a blow. Finally, with tremendous effort he made himself say, "It's wonderful to see you after—after all this time. I missed—I missed you so much . . ." The words trailed off uncertainly.

She said, clearly, "I don't think my mother would like you to be here."

"No," he said. "No, I guess she wouldn't." He clenched his fist, crumpling the hat he still held in his hand. The headmistress was right: This wasn't fair to the child. This reappearance of a father who had been a disgrace, a drunkard. This stranger who once had frightened and humiliated her. No, it wasn't fair; it was expecting too much.

He said, "I'm sorry, Lisa," and went quickly out of the room, closing the door.

The headmistress was sitting at her desk; and seeing the compassion in her face, he felt an impulse to spare her, to make the whole sorry business easier for her if he could. He said, "It's all right. I don't blame her. I'm sorry if I've upset her—or you. I'll be going now."

She stood up slowly and looked at him thoughtfully. "The front door may be locked by now, Mr. Caldwell. Will you come this way?"

She led him down a corridor, through a small chapel, down yet another passage. At the end, she turned to him, her hand on the doorknob. "I heard what Lisa said to you, Mr. Caldwell. But sometimes, you know, when children are startled or confused, they don't know what to say or do. Sometimes it takes them a little time to readjust . . . They . . ."

"I know." He didn't want to stay, to discuss, to probe and analyze. "Thank you." He just wanted to get away, to forget, to drown . . .

She moved aside. "I think you can find your way from here."

He opened the door, stepped across the threshold, and stopped. He was back in the room with Lisa. He had come through the far door. The headmistress had led him through the corridors and the chapel only to bring him back to this room.

The child was standing near one of the windows, her forehead pressed against the glass. She was making no sound, but her shoulders were quivering. He waited until he knew his voice would be steady. Then he said, "I'm still here, Lisa."

She whirled and came running blindly toward him, head thrown back, mouth twisted, tears bright on her face. He knelt and caught her quickly, feeling the thin childish arms tighten around his neck, lock themselves, and cling to him as if they would never let him go. Her heart was hammering as if it would burst the fragile cage of her body. "Oh, Daddy . . . Daddy . . . Daddy."

He had no words to offer. He simply held her, feeling the love and gratitude pour through him like a mighty river, washing it all away, the barren days and empty nights, the soul sickness, the despair. Behind him he heard the door close gently, but the sound did not frighten him now. Not now. Not any more. Not ever again.

XXI

Sometimes I think life is rather like a movie, a succession of still pictures flashing by so fast that you get the illusion of endless motion and action. Well, not quite endless, of course. At some point each of us has to come to the final frame, the last picture where the camera stops turning for good.

A somber notion, really; no one likes to dwell on it. But once or twice I've found myself experiencing something so unusual, so breathless, so exquisite that the thought has crossed my mind: *If there has to be a final moment, a final memory, you couldn't do much better than this.*

I remember thinking that once in a South Carolina duck blind on an icy winter morning just before sunrise. When I remember it now, it's still so vivid that it all comes back in the present tense:

Bob Sprague, my oldest friend, and I tramping along the muddy embankment that is part of the old rice plantation. In the east the first pale smears of dawn. All around us the dark, brooding expanse of marsh. Overhead the frosty glitter of the stars.

Tuffy, Bob's sweet-tempered Labrador, leads the way, tail wagging furiously, nose picking up marvelous scents of rabbit, raccoon, fox, heaven knows what. Now the flashlight's wavering finger falls on the canoe upside down on the bank, bottom shining with dew, decoys stacked underneath. One paddler in the bow, one in the stern. Tuffy—shivering more with excitement than cold—amidships. Then the silent passage through black and silver shadows, Venus so bright that she looks like a diamond stickpin in the scarf of night, her reflection dancing in the ripples that arrow away from the bow. Our paddles make almost no sound. Somewhere upwind a mallard hen quacks sleepily. An unseen flight of teal or widgeon takes off with a rush of wings.

The blind, thatched with reeds and palmetto, looms ahead. The canoe lurches as Tuffy flings himself out and flounders happily toward it. The eastern sky blazes with crimson. The decoys fall with subdued splashes and swing into position, bobbing solemnly. High overhead there is the thin sweet whistle of wing feathers combing the wind. The ducks are moving, now. It's still too early to shoot. We must wait for the legal time.

So we wait, fingers numb, breaths steaming in the frosty air. The blind faces west. On the horizon, straight ahead of us, is a heavy cloud bank. And suddenly, as the sun clears the rim of the world, a magnificent rainbow arches against this dark backdrop. We stare in silence, and as we stare another rainbow, even higher, shimmers into view above the first. And in between these stupendous bands of color, and through them, and around them, the ducks are flying, spears of golden light flashing now on their underwings as they draw their exquisite traceries through luminous air.

Well . . .

In the story that follows, Conroy wanted a memory like this. But he had a special reason.

A Reason for Living

All the way across the bleak, wind-chopped bay, Conroy had seemed in high spirits. He stood silhouetted against the sunset, a bulky figure in his hunting clothes, braced against the frenzied bucking of the powerboat. Bannister sat huddled amidships, trying not to be frightened. Only a moderate sea was running, but to a man unfamiliar with salt water, a man who could barely swim, the steel-gray waves looked enormous, menacing.

Bannister hung on grimly and wondered for the fiftieth time why Mike Conroy had asked him on a duck-shooting trip. They were good friends, but Bannister was no hunter. He had never shot a duck in his life. Still, Conroy had talked him into it, and here they were in the middle of Barnegat Bay on a freezing December afternoon with night coming down over a wilderness of marsh and water.

A wave slapped them and the air was full of tiny liquid pellets so cold they seemed to burn the skin. Bannister winced, but Conroy whipped off his shooting cap and shook his grizzled, leonine head as if he loved it. He said something to Bill Keller, the leathery-faced bayman at the wheel. Keller pointed, and Conroy turned his head. "You can see it now, Charlie. Your hotel for the night."

Half a mile away a crazy silhouette was etched dimly against the western sky. It was a shack built on stilts rising eight or ten feet above the marsh. A skeleton dock led down to the water.

Bannister said, incredulously, "We sleep in that?"

Conroy clapped him jovially on the shoulder. "It's a lot more comfortable than it looks. You'll see."

Ten minutes later the powerboat nosed up to the dock. The bluster of the engine died. The sudden silence was like a blow.

"Come on, Charlie," Conroy said. "We'll get a fire going while Bill unloads the gear." He strode confidently along the narrow catwalk. "Mind you don't slip; there's ice on these planks."

Bannister followed slowly, trying to shake off the depression that was settling over him. He had never been particularly moody, or sensitive to environments. But this frozen, lonely place . . .

Inside the shack, Conroy was lighting an oil lamp. "Come in, come in!" he said.

The shack was about twelve feet square. Double-decker bunks with red blankets occupied two corners. A table and four chairs stood in the middle of the floor. There was a kerosene burner for cooking, a sink with a drain but no running water, and at the far end a large Franklin stove. There were shelves of tinned goods, half a dozen old magazines, and some well-thumbed playing cards. It was bitterly cold; Bannister saw all this through the fog of his own breath.

Conroy touched a match to the fire already laid in the big stove. "It'll warm up in no time." He looked up as Keller came in with the guns and rucksacks. "That's fine, Bill. Thanks."

"How about tomorrow, Mr. Conroy?" the bayman asked.

The big man hesitated, frowning. "You'd better come over about ten in the morning. If we have no luck, we won't want to sit out here all day."

Keller nodded. "Don't think you'll want to quit that early. But I'll come just the same. Good luck to you."

He backed out and closed the door. A moment later they heard the whine of the engine. Bannister moved to a window and watched the boat curve away. Silence settled down again, complete, profound. "My God," Bannister said, "it's really the middle of nowhere, isn't it?"

Conroy was unpacking the rucksacks. "It's isolated, all right. But that's what I like about it. No problems out here." He was silent for a moment. "Except the ones you bring with you."

Something in his voice, some flatness that had not been there before, made Bannister wheel around suddenly. "What made you invite me, Mike? I know at least six of our friends who'd give their eyeteeth to be out here with you. I don't know a mallard from a teal, but you practically shanghaied me! Provided these clothes, a gun, everything. Why?"

Conroy finished one rucksack and started methodically on

the other. "I like you, for one thing, Charlie. And I think you like me."

"Of course I like you! We've been friends for years. You've helped me over some rough spots, and I'm grateful. But I'm puzzled by all this. There's something behind it, isn't there?"

"Maybe," said Conroy. "Maybe. But let me get to it in my own time, will you? Meanwhile—,"he gave Bannister a rather forced smile—, "how about some supper?"

They had supper. They washed the dishes. They sat at the table in the yellow light and played gin rummy. Outside, night gripped the cabin in an icy fist. The wind was rising; it moaned eerily across the frozen marsh. Now and then heavy gusts smote the cabin, making the lamps flicker.

Bannister found it difficult to concentrate on his cards. Try as he would, he could not banish the conviction that something unpleasant, something sinister lay ahead of him. And yet, he told himself, such premonitions were ridiculous. He had known Conroy for twenty years—the man was as sound as the bank he controlled. Everyone admired him: a fine sportsman, a solid citizen, an excellent host. A widower with two grown children, both married. Never a breath of scandal, never a hint of anything shady or dishonest. A loyal friend, sympathetic and generous. Why, a year ago when Bannister had applied for a loan and the bank turned him down for lack of sufficient collateral, Conroy had let him have thirty thousand on a simple personal note—no security at all.

Could it be, Bannister wondered, something to do with that personal loan? Hardly. The note wasn't due for another six months. And even if it were overdue, why an expedition into this improbable place to discuss it? It made no sense. There must be something else; there had to be . . .

The wind pounced down again, the shack seemed to shrink; the windows rattled. Bannister thought of the ducks huddled in the freezing marshes waiting for the dawn, and involuntarily he shivered.

"What's the matter?" Conroy asked him. "Cold?"

"No. Somebody walked over my grave, I guess."

"Not superstitious, are you?"

"No. It's just an old saying."

"I'm glad you're not superstitious," Conroy said grimly. "That *would* have been a bore!"

Bannister was puzzled. "What do you mean?"

Conroy ignored the question. He said, after a pause, "Remember that dinner party at the Emmetts', Charlie? Four, five months ago?"

"Sure," Bannister said. "It was a good evening."

"Recall that discussion we all had after dinner?"

"No. Not particularly."

Conroy drew a card and discarded it. "It was about mercy killing. Euthanasia."

"Oh, yes." Bannister also made a discard. "We did talk about that, didn't we?"

"Several points of view were expressed," Conroy said slowly. "I particularly remember yours. You said you thought that no doctor had the right to take a human life without the consent of the patient. But if the patient were fully aware of the situation, and requested the needle, then you thought he was entitled to have it. Isn't that what you said?"

"I don't remember exactly," Bannister said. "It's quite possible that I did." He indicated the deck of cards. "Your turn, Mike."

Conroy's big hand came out and took a card. He said, without changing his inflection, "I have terminal cancer, Charlie. The doctors say I won't last more than six months."

Bannister sat quite still; his face looked suddenly pinched and drawn.

"Six months," Conroy repeated. He inserted the card into his hand carefully. "Not a very pleasant six months, either. About two more months of relative normalcy. Then two more on opiates. Then two more during which not even the opiates will help—much." He laid down his cards, face up, and stared at Bannister. "Gin!"

Bannister swallowed hard. "My God, Mike, I don't know what to say! Are you absolutely sure?"

Conroy made an impatient gesture. "Don't worry. I had the diagnosis checked. And rechecked. There's no doubt about it."

"But can't they do something? Can't they operate—try x-ray? Do *something?*"

"Could have," Conroy said coolly, "a year ago. I waited too long, Charlie. Like a damn fool. But I never thought the symptoms I had were important . . ." He held out the cards. "Another hand?"

Bannister brushed them aside. "Look, Mike," he said earnestly. "I know a doctor who's a specialist. One of the very best. When we go back tomorrow, I'll phone him first thing. He . . ."

"Thanks, Charlie," Conroy said. "But I'm not going back tomorrow."

"What do you mean?"

Conroy looked straight into his eyes. "You know exactly what I mean." He got up and began to pace to and fro. "I've thought about it very carefully, Charlie—ever since I knew. It's the only thing that makes sense, under the circumstances. I've had a good life, a full life. Why let it end in misery and agony?"

Bannister said nothing.

"It's not as if I were needed anywhere," Conroy went on. "Both the kids are married—they have their own lives. The bank will survive, Lord knows. My friends may miss me briefly, but no more than they would if I waited six months."

Bannister wet his lips. "You never know . . ."

"Some miraculous cure, you mean? Don't be silly, Charlie! They won't find one in the next six months, and even if they did it would be too late to do me any good." He wheeled back to the table and put his hands flat on it. "You said it yourself, Charlie, that night at the Emmetts'. You said that while man has nothing to say about his arrival in this world, he does control his exit from it! You said that if an incurable patient, facing great pain, asked his doctor for a lethal needle, he was entitled to it. You said that, don't deny it! Well . . ." he straightened up slowly, "I'm the patient, Charlie. And you're the doctor. And this—," he picked up the shotgun, balancing it in his big hand—, "this is the needle."

"No!" Bannister pushed back his chair. "It would be murder!"

"Not at all," said Conroy calmly. "It will be an accident. Look." He sat down again, smiling a little, like a teacher explaining something simple to a rather backward pupil. "You asked me earlier why I chose you for this expedition. Two reasons, Charlie. First: the things you said that night at the Emmetts'. Second: the fact that you've never been duck shooting. Anybody knows that an inexperienced man is dangerous in a duck blind. It's easy to get excited, rattled. You start swinging on a bird and you forget to stop, that's all. Happens every year. No, don't interrupt for a minute."

He put out one hand and pressed Bannister back into his chair. "It will be an *accident.* No one will even question it. Oh, there'll be an inquest and all that, but you'll be cleared automatically. People will feel sorry for you, but they'll soon forget it. And you'll have the satisfaction of knowing that you've rendered a very great service to a friend."

"No!" said Bannister again. "You're crazy, Mike! I couldn't do a thing like that!"

Conroy kept on smiling. "Just what I thought you'd say at first. It's the normal reaction, the conventional one. But before we're through I think I can make you see it differently." He actually laughed. "After all, you've got to listen. You can't run away, unless you want to row over to the mainland."

Bannister calmed himself with an effort. "Listen, Mike, why don't you . . ."

"Why don't I just eat some sleeping pills and get it over with? Well, I'll tell you, Charlie, I did think of that. I thought of it very seriously. But, my God, what a dull way to go! And then, rightly or wrongly, there's a certain stigma attached to suicide. I didn't want the other kids pointing at my grandchildren and whispering. No. I said to myself, 'Look, Conroy, if you could arrange things so that the exact moment of your death coincided with a moment of great happiness what would that moment be?' And then, of course, I knew it would be the moment in which I've just nailed a pair of incoming ducks, right and left, a good clean double. My mind would be so full of excitement and satisfaction there'd be no room for anything else. If oblivion came then, I told myself, that would be fine, that would be perfect." He leaned back in his chair. "So here we are, Charlie. Here we are."

There was a silence in which Bannister could hear the rusty alarm clock tick. Finally he said, "And if I refuse?"

Conroy shrugged. "I can't force you, of course. I'll have to arrange it somehow myself. A clumsy business, which will fool no one. And I must say, I don't relish the thought of it. But . . ." he clenched his fist slowly . . . "I'm not going back tomorrow, Charlie. This thing is going to be settled by the time Bill Keller gets over here at ten o'clock. One way or the other."

He stood up again and moved over to the window. "Wind's hauling around to the northeast. They should be flying tomorrow, all right." He turned slowly. "I've left all my affairs in pretty good shape, Charlie. Not too perfect—I didn't want it to look as if I'd planned on stepping out of the picture. And while I was at it, I dug this out of the safe." He tossed a folded paper on the table. "That's your note, Charlie. I've marked it 'Paid in Full.'"

Bannister looked down at the paper. He did not touch it.

"I hope you won't consider it a bribe," Conroy said. "It's just that—well, I know you need the money, and I don't. So tear it up, if you like. Or keep it for the record, whichever you prefer." He stretched his hands above his head and yawned. "What say we hit the sack? Five o'clock'll be on us before we know it." He slapped Bannister roughly on the shoulder. "Forget all this morbid stuff for now. Don't think of it again until we're in the blind. Or, if you've got to think of it, just figure I did you a couple of favors once, and now you're going to pay me back. As for me," Conroy rubbed his chin reflectively, "I'm all through with thinking. I'm just going to dream about ducks, that's all."

He sat down on the edge of one of the bunks, pulled off his boots, peeled his clothes down to his heavy underwear. "Don't bother to set the alarm clock," he said. "I always wake up. Haven't missed in thirty years."

He rolled over and pulled the blankets around him. Bannister sat very still, staring at the canceled note. Outside, the wind seemed to have dropped a bit, but the cabin creaked with

171

cold. In the silence the clock ticked loudly, and suddenly Bannister noticed another sound, gentle, rhythmical.

It was Conroy, snoring.

The blind was on a small island in the bay perhaps a third of a mile from the cabin. It faced due west, an almost invisible slit in the frozen marsh. Near it was a tiny cove, and into this Conroy drove the rowboat. "Here we are," he said. "Just about right. It'll be light enough to shoot in ten minutes."

He steadied the rowboat while Bannister stepped out, then dragged it into the stiff, brittle grass. A camouflaged skiff was lying there, decoys stacked neatly in the stern. Conroy shoved it into the water. "I'll rig out. You can get set in the blind, if you want to."

Bannister said nothing. He had hardly spoken a word since the night before. He picked up the guns and rucksacks and carried them to the blind. As he did so, two shadowy projectiles flashed over his head. "Pintail," said Conroy, balancing in the skiff. "Look at 'em go!"

Bannister watched him toss the decoys, each one hitting with a subdued splash, bobbing a bit, then coming to rest. Light was filtering rapidly into the sky now. There was just enough wind to riffle the steely water. It was piercingly cold. Inside his heavy gloves, Bannister's fingers felt numb.

Conroy poled the skiff to shore, dragged it up, covered it with marsh grass. He jumped down into the blind and looked at Bannister. "We've got plenty of time," he said. "Let's see how it goes for a while, eh?"

"Look, Mike," Bannister began.

He felt the other's hand pressing him down. "Here comes a single now! Gun loaded? No? Well, maybe I can nail him." There was a metallic snick as Conroy broke his gun and jammed in two shells. The duck, a big Canadian redleg, drove straight for the decoys, set his wings, then flared as Conroy stood up. The twelve-gauge roared once; the bird fell. "Splashed that one," said Conroy happily.

He stood there, tense and eager; Bannister thought he had never seen a man more alive. "Might as well get him before he drifts away," Conroy said. He climbed out of the blind, dragged the skiff into the water, poled out rapidly and retrieved the bird. "Load up, load up," he said when he got back. "You'll get a shot in a minute."

"Mike," said Bannister imploringly. "Mike, I've got to talk to you. I—"

"No!" Conroy whirled on him; for the first time his face looked angry. "No more talking! Some time this morning I'm going to turn my back on you and try to kill a pair of ducks. Then it's up to you. If you fail me, I'll do it myself, understand? But I don't want to talk about it. This is my last hunt; I'm not going to have it spoiled by a lot of gloomy chatter. Look there!" He pointed. "Here comes a flight of butterballs. They won't decoy; they'll go right over us." He picked up Bannister's gun, loaded it, thrust it into his hands. "Let's see you tag one!"

Bannister hesitated, then fired both barrels almost simultaneously into what seemed a solid mass of feathers. The recoil staggered him, he hadn't realized how a twelve-gauge could kick. But no bird fell.

"Shot at the whole flock, didn't you?" Conroy said. He laughed. "Almost never hit anything when you do that. Pick one bird, even if you can see twenty. You'll get another chance in a minute."

But the minutes passed and nothing happened. Behind them the sky turned crimson; the sun rose. The wind picked up; ragged clouds began to scud across the sky. It grew even colder; ice bearded the decoys and crept along the edges of the marsh. Several flights went by, but none of the birds seemed interested in the decoys.

"Look," Conroy said uneasily at last. "We may not get as many chances as I thought. We'd better get our little affair settled, Charlie. Next time a bird comes in, hey?" His hand gripped Bannister's knee with a quick pressure. "Bless you, old man. Good luck, always."

Bannister said nothing. He stared straight ahead of him at the bobbing decoys. His gun stood in the righthand corner of the blind, loaded, ready. A faint rime of frost had formed on the barrels. The twin muzzles stared into the sky, sightless, ominous.

Conroy said suddenly, "There's a pair of blacks. Coming up the bay!"

Bannister looked to his left. He watched the two specks in the sky drive nearer, beating up against the wind. He saw them dip toward the decoys, then swing out again. The great hand that seemed to be squeezing his heart relaxed momentarily, then tightened again as the birds veered abruptly toward the blind. Conroy looked at him once; his face was tight and grim. "Get set," he said.

Bannister slipped off his gloves and reached for the gun. The metal was so cold that it seemed to stick to his fingers. Conroy turned away from him in a half crouch. The birds came driving in from the left, high. When they were eighty yards away, Conroy clicked off his safety. Seventy yards. Sixty. Conroy's muscles tensed. And then the birds flared out. Something had made them suspicious. They passed the blind just out of range. Bannister heard his own breath go out of him in a whistling sigh. He could see it vaporing in the icy air, but he was sweating. He said in a choked whisper, "Mike—"

"Keep still," Conroy muttered. "Keep down. They're coming back!"

It was true. The ducks were swinging downwind in a great circle. They had decided there was no danger. They were going to make another pass.

They came in low and fast. Sixty yards away they set their wings. On they came over the restless water as if drawn by invisible wires. Fifty yards. Forty. Thirty-five.

Conroy stood up. The twelve-gauge bellowed; the lead duck collapsed in a bundle of feathers. The second mallard flared high, backpedaling. The wind caught him and whisked him away. Conroy's second barrel slammed; the bird faltered, one wing dropped, and it plunged into the bay. Conroy stood rigid, his back to Bannister, waiting. The wind blew. The silence screamed around them.

Slowly Conroy turned his head. His face was gray; a trickle of blood ran down his chin from a bitten lip. "Blast you," he said in a hoarse, shaking voice. "Blast you, Charlie."

Bannister held up his gun slowly. "The safety," he said in a voice that he no longer recognized as his own. "I forgot to take off the safety."

Conroy's eyes moved from Bannister's sweating face down to the safety catch, then back again. He said, "You're lying, Charlie."

"No," Bannister said. "You'll see. Next time." He began to climb stiffly out of the blind, holding his gun in one hand.

"Where are you going?" Conroy's eyes were narrowed.

"Your second bird," Bannister said. "Only crippled."

He pointed. The duck, wing tipped, was swimming strongly away.

"Let it go," said Conroy.

"No," said Bannister. "No, I'll get it."

He launched the skiff and stepped in, feeling it lurch under his weight. He raised the long pole and drove it forward. His first thrusts were easy, the water was shallow. Then the bottom shelved off steeply and he could barely reach it. Ahead of him he could see the duck, head flattened, snaking through the water. He picked up his gun and held it an inch or so from his shoulder. He did not bother to aim. He leaned back slightly and pulled the trigger. The gun slammed hard against his shoulder. He felt the skiff slide from under him. For a long moment he seemed to hang in the air. Then the water seized him.

He had thought himself prepared for the shock. He was wrong. The cold was beyond belief. It struck him like a hammer, numbing yet agonizing. His legs were instantly paralyzed. He thrashed once or twice with his arms, then they too ceased to function.

A pocket of air, trapped under his hunting jacket, gave him momentary buoyancy. Far away, dimly, he heard Conroy's bull voice roaring something—instructions, encouragement—he did not know which. Or care. A curious languor crept over him. The cold no longer bothered him. He felt almost warm. He went under, mouth open, and an icy stream of water poured into his lungs. The pain, sharp and piercing, roused him and he began to struggle feebly. But now his sodden clothes were giving up their air cells. His boots had filled; they dragged him down. His hand touched something hard; his fingers curled around it in agony. The pole. It gave him a partial support that seemed to his tortured mind worse than no support at all. He tried to let it go, to sink, to be at rest, but his fingers would not relax. They were rigid, immovable, a frozen claw riveted around the length of oak.

For an eternity he wallowed miserably; his brain reeling. And then, with a crash that seemed to split his skull, something thudded alongside. A giant hand gripped his hair, then his collar. He felt himself dragged in one agonizing wrench from the numbing embrace of the bay. Conroy dropped him on the floor of the rowboat and lunged for the oars, which were sliding away. He was roaring something at Bannister, but the words made no sense. The rowboat seemed to be spinning like a top. Bannister lay on the floorboards, shivering and retching. He had no will to live anymore. He wanted to die.

Incredibly, Conroy's big boot flicked out and caught him in the ribs. Hard. Conroy's words began to penetrate his numbed brain. "Get up!" Conroy was howling. "You'll freeze to death lying there. Get up and row! Get up, I say!"

Bannister shook his head. "Let me alone," he gasped. "Let me alone!"

Conroy leaned down and slapped his face. "Get up!" He put his hands under Bannister's armpits and raised him to a sitting position. He shook him until the icy spray flew from his hair. "Row!" he screamed. He dragged Bannister to a sitting position on the thwart, forced the oar handles under his blue fingers, then knelt behind him, his own hands covering Bannister's. He threw his weight back; the oars bit deep into the seething water. "Row!"

"I can't," Bannister moaned. His hands were on fire. Every movement was agony. "Let me alone. Let me die."

"Die?" howled Conroy. "You're going to live, if I have to kill you! You're going to *live!*"

Afterwards, in the superheated cabin, from under a mound of blankets Bannister said feebly, "I tried to tell you last night, Mike. And I tried again this morning. You just wouldn't listen."

Conroy was pouring out a steaming cup of coffee. "Tell me what?"

"That nobody can be sure they're not needed. That *that's* the reason for going on living, right up to the end. You saved a life today, two minutes after you planned to end your own. You can't say you weren't needed out there just now, can you?"

Conroy took a spoon out of the table drawer. "No, I can't say that." He stirred the drink slowly. "Tell the truth, I never thought of it quite that way, Charlie. Too busy thinking about myself, I guess."

He came over to the bunk and stood looking down at his friend. He said softly, "You didn't *plan* to fall overboard, did you, Charlie. Just to prove your point, I mean?"

The man under the blankets smiled faintly. "Nobody would be *that* foolish, would they, Mike?"

"I don't know," Conroy said. "I guess I'll never know."

Bannister took the cup from him with a hand that was mottled but fairly steady. He drank some, then put the cup on the floor. He settled back and closed his eyes. "How about it, Mike? Did I make my point?"

Conroy was looking out of the window at the windswept bay. Pretty soon, he knew, Bill Keller would be coming to pick them up. "You try to get some sleep, Charlie," he said. "I'll stick around."

XXII

The world is full of questions which have no answers. What is gravity, for example; how does it work? What is aging; why do we grow old? How old is the universe; ten billion years? Fifteen? Twenty? Did it all really start with a big bang? If so, what preceded that?

The existence of evil in the world—how to account for it? Seems to me you can't really say that it exists outside of or contrary to the will of God—if you believe that you are really believing in two opposing Gods. No, God evidently permits the existence of evil for reasons that we can't understand. Stretches the mind to think about it, but it's beyond our reach.

I knew a young doctor once whose fiancée died. He seemed very bitter for a while, and it was hard to blame him, because the death of a young person—to our short sight, anyway—seems like a cruel deprivation. I found myself wondering how such a person would deal with his bitterness, what might happen that would diminish or neutralize it. *What if*, I said to myself, *what if it all worked out like this?*

The Answer

At seven-thirty on that cool October morning, Dr. Rodney Morgan came out of the towering mass of gray stone that was the hospital. He stood for a moment in the pale sunlight, a slender young man with reddish hair, tired eyes, a twenty-four-hour beard. His shoulders sagged; he looked like a man who had taken a beating. Which was not surprising; he *had* been beaten—by the oldest adversary of all.

A taxi went by, tires singing on the damp pavement. A girl was in it, quite a pretty girl. Alive, vibrant, plunging into the mystery and excitement of a new day. Rod Morgan watched the taxi until it swung around a corner, out of sight. On that corner stood a church, its soaring spire sharp against the deep autumnal blue. Slowly he clenched his fist. "You make no sense," he said to it aloud. "The whole damned universe makes no sense."

With fingers that shook a little, he lit a cigarette, drew on it once, then flung it away. He went down to the street where his car stood in the space reserved for doctors. It was only nine hours since he had left it there. It seemed more like nine years.

The engine caught instantly with a comforting purr. "An old car," he had said to Marilyn once, "is like an old friend—much more satisfactory than a new one." And Marilyn had cried, tossing her burnished hair in the eager way she had, "Oh, I agree! And especially if it's a convertible. A convertible is so much more—more *human*, don't you think?"

Now that clear young voice would speak no more. Not to him. Not to anyone.

Don't think about it, he said to himself. *Later, maybe, but not now. Not now . . .*

The almost empty streets fled past; the great snarling city was not yet fully awake. Only three weeks ago, celebrating her nineteenth birthday, he had taken Marilyn dancing. It had been late, very late, when he had finally taken her home. Driving slowly, with her head on his shoulder, he had said, "You know, if you grow up any more, I'll have to ask you to marry me." And she had said, "I'll keep right on taking my vitamins, Dr. Morgan."

He clenched his teeth, trying not to remember, holding back the wild surges of grief and fury and despair. Giving in to them would do no good. Nothing would do any good. *Marilyn. Marilyn . . .*

He came to his apartment building and let himself into the small bachelor flat. The shower was warm; the clean strokes of the razor were welcome. But he could eat no breakfast, and when he lay down on his bed, he knew that he would not be able to sleep, either.

He got up and moved over to the window. Far below, at the end of the street, he could see a segment of the river sparkling with a hard, merry light. How tranquil that river, how serene, how unaffected by human suffering. There it flowed, placid and unheeding, just as it had on countless occasions when he and Marilyn . . . *No, don't think about it. Everything possible was done. These things happen, medically . . .*

Somewhere church bells began to ring, and he remembered with a faint shock of surprise that it was Sunday. In the dark hours of the night he had lost track of time completely. Well, if it was Sunday, he need not stay here. He had some telephone calls to make, but they could wait. He would drive out of the city, get away by himself, try to forget about it all.

He turned from the window, dressed quickly. As he opened the apartment door, the telephone rang. He stood there, motionless, his face set and grim. Somewhere in this teeming concrete hive a patient was calling him, calling for help in the endless human struggle against pain, suffering, disease. But what difference did it make? The deck was stacked, the dice were loaded from the beginning. In the end, death always won.

"Go on, ring," said Rod Morgan and went out quickly, closing the door behind him.

Over one of the silver bridges he drove, out through the suburbs with their neat lawns and piles of burning leaves, on into rolling country where the lemon-colored sun shone steadily and a blue haze shimmered on the distant hills. He had had no conscious destination in mind, but soon he became aware that the car was following a familiar set of roads. He let it take the right turnings until at last he came to Leedville.

Drowsing in its Sunday-morning calm, the little town looked just the same. In two years, nothing had changed. There were the same elms; the same shops; the same garages, churches, restaurants; the same Civil War cannon rusting peacefully on the village green. Here Rod Morgan had spent twelve months after completing his internship, twelve memorable months as assistant to Hobart Merriman, M.D. An old country sawbones—that was the label Hobe gave himself disparagingly. All the same, in one year Rod Morgan had learned more from him than he had learned in all the years before—or since.

Like a horse that knows its stable, the car turned down a side street. It stopped before the familiar weathered house. Rod Morgan got out, pushed back the creaking gate, walked up the path, pressed the bell. When the door opened, he said, "Hello, Hobe."

The old doctor took the pipe out of his mouth and stared. "By Gadfrey." A hand like a steel clamp fastened itself on the visitor's shoulder. "Rod! Rod, boy! By Gadfrey, it's good to see you!"

Rodney Morgan said, "It's good to be here."

"Come in, come in!" Hobe Merriman swung wide the door. "I've got some coffee going in the office." The stocky figure moved through the dim hallway. "By Gadfrey, this is a pleasant surprise! When you rang, I thought it'd be old Martha Sturgis with a new set of imaginary symptoms. Ha! Remember her? She asks about you now and then. Sort of wistfully—I guess you used to give her more sympathy than I do."

He pushed open the door that led to the office and that, too, was just the same—the quiet street outside, the blended smells of coffee and old leather, of antiseptics and tobacco, Hobe's big old-fashioned cluttered desk, his ancient swivel chair. Here were all the good things—kindness and gentleness, wisdom and tolerance, patience and skill. But instead of reassuring Rod Morgan, instead of steadying him, awareness of them seemed to weaken him, to lower the barriers of self-control, so that for half a second he thought he was going to cry.

He sank his teeth into his lower lip, and as he did so, the blue eyes behind the steel-rimmed glasses looked up at him. "What's the matter, boy?" Then, after a moment of silence, the infallible instinct went close to the heart of the trouble. "Lose a patient?"

The younger man nodded. The old doctor turned, took a cup and saucer from a shelf, poured a stream of black and steaming brew. "You don't take sugar, as I remember." He handed it over. He said, in the same even tone, "Want to talk about it?"

Rod Morgan took the coffee. "I don't know if I can, Hobe. I just feel sick. Sick and miserable. And bitter."

The swivel chair creaked as Hobe Merriman sat down. "Maybe you'd better not keep it locked up inside, then."

Staring at his untouched coffee, Rod Morgan told the story. At the end, he said, "We tried everything, Hobe. Everything. Nothing did any good. It—it wasn't so much the fact that medical science failed; we know that has to happen, sometimes. It was just that—that I *loved* her, Hobe. I loved her more, even, than I knew. When I—when I saw that she was going, I tried to call her back. I tried to hold her with my love. It was the strongest thing I . . ." He shook his head. "It was no good. All that love made no difference."

Hobe Merriman struck a match and relit his pipe. He said nothing.

Rod Morgan stood up and moved over to the fireplace. He put his coffee cup down. He said, in a low voice, "If love is powerless, Hobe, then why bother, why knock yourself out, why try so hard? It can mean only one thing, really: that the whole business—life, death, everything—is nothing but a big clumsy machine that somehow got wound up and left to run. It doesn't care what happens, or who gets hurt, because it has no meaning. It has no heart!"

Hobe Merriman put his pipe down. "You can't think like that, Rod, and be a doctor. Not a good one, anyway."

"Marilyn's dead, isn't she?" Rod Morgan swung around furiously. "Why? Give me one good reason why! You can't, and you know it!" He slammed his hand suddenly against the wall. "Don't you ever get sick of being a faithful mechanic, of just patching up nature's mistakes? Don't you ever ask yourself *why*? Why all this suffering? Why all this pain? Why? . . ."

"If there were no pain," said Dr. Merriman, "we'd be in a fine mess. No diagnosis, half the time. No warning. Besides, without pain, how would people value pleasure?"

Rod Morgan shook his head. "That's not good enough, Hobe. Oh, it's good as far as it goes. But some things just seem like senseless cruelty. Not only Marilyn's death. There were things that happened when I was here with you, plenty of them. That baby of Katherine West's, remember? The hydro-cephalus one?"

Dr. Merriman nodded.

"Well, there was a mother with an idiot child, a baby doomed from the moment it was born. Do you remember how she fought for that poor abnormal creature, how she prayed? Len Thomas down at the Episcopal church told me that she came in every single day, month after month, and prayed—prayed at the altar rail—that her child might be well and whole. And what happened?"

Still Dr. Merriman said nothing.

Rod Morgan said flatly, "The child must have died soon after I left. It did die, didn't it?"

"Yes," said Hobe Merriman, "the child died."

"Well, how did that leave you feeling? How did you fit that case into your concept of a universe that makes sense?"

Hobe Merriman took off his glasses and polished them with the end of his tie. He started to speak and thought better of it. Finally he glanced at his watch. "Let's walk down to the hospital, shall we? I took out old Mike Murphy's gall bladder yesterday. Might as well see if it left him as ornery as ever."

Rod Morgan took a deep breath. "All right, Hobe."

They went out of the house together and walked slowly through the gilded streets. "Indian summer," Hobe Merriman said. "Mighty pleasant time of year."

"I'm sorry, Hobe," the younger man said. "When I left the city this morning, I had no intention of coming out here to cry on your shoulder. Believe me, I didn't."

"I'm glad you came," the old doctor said. "I know what you're going through, Rod. I've been through it more than once myself. It's hell while it lasts. It's like having a hole bored in you, and through the hole all your courage and faith seem to drain away."

Rod Morgan looked up at the polished blue of the sky. "Faith? Faith in what?"

They came to the hospital, a small building, but modern and well-equipped. They went up the steps, along the polished corridors. Outside a door marked NO ADMITTANCE, Dr. Merriman stopped. "We've changed things around a bit since you were here. Come on in; I've got something to show you."

Rod Morgan stepped across the threshold and found himself in a warm, softly lighted room facing a row of tiny cribs. His companion took two sterile gowns and masks from a shelf, tossed one set to Rod and shrugged himself into the other. He moved over to the third crib from the end and scooped up the occupant expertly. He held out the tiny bundle. "What do you think of this young lady?"

For the first time that day, Rod Morgan smiled. "With those eyelashes, she'll be a heartbreaker some day."

"She's more than pretty. She's perfect. Here, hold her a minute."

Rod Morgan took the sleeping child, touched her cheek gently, "What's her name?"

"They're calling her after her mother," Hobe Merriman said. "Her name is Katherine West."

He leaned back, stocky shoulders braced against the wall, hands jammed deep into his pockets. "The mother prayed that her child might be well and whole—remember?—and the child died. But she kept on living; she didn't give up. Now she has another child that *is* well and whole. Who's to say her prayers weren't answered?"

The baby stirred in Rod Morgan's arms; a clenched fist no bigger than his thumb described a sleepy circle and was still again.

"That's your answer, Rod," the old doctor said. "The only answer God gives us, really. Courage to keep going, no matter what happens to you. Faith in the universe, even when it seems to make no sense. That's the deepest faith of all. And the reward is what you're holding in your arms. The reward is life itself."

Under the gauze mask, Rod Morgan bit his lip suddenly. He said nothing.

"I'd better go and see my patient," Hobe Merriman said. "But it's odd, your coming here at just this time. It's odd, your mentioning Katherine West. Coincidence? Maybe. I don't know. Do you?"

Rod Morgan shook his head. Carefully, tenderly, he put the baby back into the crib. Looking down at her, he said, "I walked out on a call when I left the city. I'd better go back."

"Stay for lunch, if you like."

He shook his head again, stripping off gown and mask.

"No. But thanks, Hobe. Thanks for everything."

"That's all right," Hobe Merriman said.

He watched the younger man stride down the corridor. Not with pity. With a little envy, perhaps. So many things to learn, so many people to help, so infinitely much to do . . .

And so much time.

XXIII

Once I heard a distinguished professor of history say that the most important and influential people in any society are not the statesmen or the economists or the engineers or the financiers; they are the poets, the painters, the architects, the sculptors, the storytellers. He said that this was true because the creative artists are in touch with and reflect realities that lie below the surface appearance of things, and these are the realities that determine the course that a culture or a society will follow.

I don't know how much truth there is in that (a lot, I'd like to think!), but I do know that the linked sequence of ideas that we call a story is one of the most effective forms of communication in the world, maybe *the* most effective. You can shout at people, argue with them, preach at them, even reason sweetly with them, and they'll turn you right off. But if you tell them a story, they'll listen.

The greatest Teacher who ever lived found the short story the surest way to reach the minds and hearts of his contemporaries. The earliest account we have of his life was probably written forty years after his death, and yet the stories he told have never faded.

What a craftsman he was! "A certain man went down from Jerusalem to Jericho and fell among thieves. . . ." Just thirteen words. But instantly you have a specific location, a central character, a crisis that demands resolution. "Which stripped him of his raiment, and wounded him, and departed, leaving him half dead. . . ." Fifteen more words: action, danger, man against death, mounting suspense. "And *then* what happened?" something in the listener cries, and is not satisfied until the Good Samaritan comes to the aid of the victim and the great moral question "Who is my neighbor?" is answered for all time.

A story doesn't have to make a profound ethical point, of course. Sometimes it can just be a once-upon-a-time thing, a fable, a dream, a legend that floats into your head from nowhere, iridescent as a soap bubble—and about as fragile.

Some years ago around Christmastime I got up very early one misty morning and walked down the path to the old falling-down dock we have that looks out over the marshes. Everything was gray and still, but I knew that when the sun came up, patches of color would flash into view all around me, and I found myself wondering idly how those little taken-for-granted visual grace notes came into being in the first place.

Later that day, as sometimes happens, a fanciful answer came floating in. I don't know which window of the magical tower would give you a view of this one, really. The skylight, maybe?

The Land Between the Rivers

Long ago, when the rivers of America were still silver, two of them flowed—not far apart—into the great sea. In those days they were nameless because there was no one to name them. No men, no women. Just the animals and birds, the trees and shrubs, and of course the wind, which was wayward and capricious, but also very wise.

One cold twilight when the days were short, the wind spoke to the animals and the birds that lived in the land between the rivers, and to the trees and the shrubs. "Tonight," the wind whispered, "you must stay awake, and watch, and wait, because a great happening may come upon you. What it will be I cannot say, because I am only the wind. But there will be a sign; this I know. When you see it, rejoice and be thankful, because after this night nothing will be the same. Stay awake, then, and be ready."

The wind sighed away into the great live oaks and across the amber marshes, and the twilight deepened, and the stars came out. The animals and the birds and the trees and the shrubs took counsel together. Most were doubtful, some were scornful. "Who can believe what is whispered by the wind?" they said. And one by one they fell asleep, the deer and the foxes, the squirrels and the shaggy bears in the swamps. Even night wanderers like the raccoons and the opossums sought their dens. The voices of the birds were stilled. They closed their bright eyes and slept.

All except one small brown bird who was troubled in his heart. "Someone must stay awake," he said to himself, "and be ready to rejoice and give thanks if this marvel does come to pass. I will wait and watch."

He sought a bush or a tree to perch in, but none of them wanted him. "We have your kind all day," they grumbled. "We need our rest at night."

But one tall green shrub took pity on the bird. "Here," it said, "I don't mind. Perch on one of my branches, and I'll stay awake and watch with you."

So the forest slept, and everything in it except the small brown bird and the tall bush, waiting. And near midnight suddenly a golden light appeared in the sky, like a mighty star, only much brighter. Silently it moved across the astonished heavens, and the bird and the bush watched until it disappeared over the rim of the world.

"Ah," they said to each other, "did you see that? How wonderful it was! How lucky we are to have seen it!" So the bird sang and the bush rustled its glossy leaves, and they gave thanks and praise in this fashion until the stars turned pale and the sun rose out of the sea.

Then all the creatures in the forest were amazed, because everywhere among the branches of the tall bush were crimson blossoms, glowing like rubies against the emerald leaves. And on the topmost twig perched a bird of flame, still singing, its scarlet plumage brighter than the sunrise.

And the wind came again and whispered to all the creatures. "See, this is the reward of faith and constancy." To the bush it murmured, "Green is the color of life and red is the color of sacrifice. Wear these hues forever." And to the bird: "Scarlet stands for the trumpet sound of courage, and for steadfastness, and for hope. Wear this badge until time is no more."

So it was, and so it still is. We call the bush the camellia, now, and the bird the cardinal. But what we call them doesn't matter, they are what they are.

This is a story that came out of the mists of the Georgia low country one year as Christmas drew near. We used to tell it around the fire when the children were small. And some of us knew that it was only a legend. But some of us believed it might be true.

Epilogue

Now it's spring here in the land between the rivers with the lovely Indian names . . . Ogeechee . . . Combahee. Outside my cabin windows azaleas flame and trees are full of the purple smoke of wisteria. The camellias are about over, but the scarlet flash of the cardinals will go on through the long hot summer.

Somehow today my mind drifts back to my earliest recollection of storytelling, earlier even than Aunt Daisy and her enchanted tower. My father is reading *A Tale of Two Cities* to my sister and me, but I am too young for it. All I can remember is a kind of drowsy contentment, listening to Father's voice going on and on, watching the firelight flicker on the brass fender in the shadowy living room, dreaming all sorts of dreams halfway between fantasy and reality.

Halfway between the imaginary and the real . . . a good place to begin. And not a bad place to end something, either. Even a book.